2008

Happy Birth
            Lenore.

You are special to me
& I don't tell you often
enough how much I
appreciate you.
    Hope you enjoy reading
            this.
                Love
                June

kisses *of* sunshine

for sisters

carol kent

kisses *of* sunshine

for sisters

ZONDERVAN™

GRAND RAPIDS, MICHIGAN 49530 USA

Kisses of Sunshine for Sisters
Copyright © 2005 by Speak Up, Inc.

Requests for information should be addressed to:
Zondervan, *Grand Rapids, Michigan 49530*

Library of Congress Cataloging-in-Publication Data

Kisses of sunshine for sisters / Carol Kent, general editor.—1st ed.
    p. cm.
    ISBN-10: 0-310-24846-9
    ISBN-13: 978-0-310-24846-0
    1. Sisters—Prayer-books and devotions—English. 2. Sisters—
Anecdotes. I. Kent, Carol, 1947–
BV4844.K57 2005
242'.643—dc22   2004022593

This edition printed on acid-free paper.

The website addresses recommended are offered as a resource to you. These websites are not intended in any way to be or imply an endorsement on the part of Zondervan, nor do we vouch for their content for the life of this book.

Published in association with the literary agency of Alive Communications, Inc., 7680 Goddard Street, Suite 200, Colorado Springs, CO 80920.

Interior design by Tracey Walker

Printed in the United States of America

05 06 07 08 09 10 11 12 /❖ DCI/ 10 9 8 7 6 5 4 3 2 1

To my four remarkable sisters:
Jennie Afman Dimkoff
Paula Afman
Bonnie Afman Emmorey
Joy Carlson

contents

introduction

*T*his *Kisses of Sunshine* series of five books — one each for sisters, moms, grandmas, teachers, and women — has lighthearted, uplifting, often humorous stories meant to bring a sunburst of joy to your life — as you remember that God loves you. My own sisters and many friends have joined me in putting these stories together. Our purpose is simply to let God's love so warm and fill you that you become warmth, light, and love to a cold, dark world.

Growing up in a home with five girls and one brother gave me a unique perspective on sisterhood. My sisters and I giggled, shared secrets, borrowed each other's clothes, had an occasional argument, made up, hugged, and carried on with daily life. In the process of growing up, we challenged each other spiritually, celebrated the births of our babies, gathered for family reunions, shared recipes, gave advice on raising strong-willed children, felt one another's hurts, divided the sorrow, multiplied the joy, and cheered when one of our sisters made it to one of life's occasional milestones.

All of my sisters are masterful storytellers. In fact, we've told each other that we have an amazing ability to make a good story *better* than what actually happened. When we get together, we often tell stories of recent experiences and then brainstorm together to find the hidden life lesson in the incident. Chris

Montaigne, in a quote on the Internet, wrote, "A sister smiles when one tells one's stories, for she knows where the decoration has been added." We hope you enjoy reading these stories as much as we enjoyed writing them.

If you have a biological sister, a sister-in-law, an adopted sister, a sister-of-the-heart, or a sister-in-the-Lord, this book is for you. I hope these stories will make you laugh out loud, encourage you to be a more creative sister, motivate you to make a difference in your world, and inspire you to deepen your faith-walk.

I'm grateful to Sandy Vander Zicht, executive editor at Zondervan, for her coaching as this series of books has been birthed. She knows women often learn more from a story than they do from a sermon, and she's been my champion during the writing and editing process.

This is a book you can read before bedtime, in the car, at the beach, or in the bathroom. Each story is a short vignette that might tickle your funny bone or move you to dry a tear. I challenge you to take a break in your busy day, pour a cup of tea or coffee (your choice), put your feet up, and read a chapter from this book. You'll be glad you did.

doin' the pinkie swing

Dawn Baker

....

The bond between sisters is unique, stretching and bending
through periods of closeness and distance,
but almost never breaking.

CAROL SALINE

My mother was only twenty-four years old when she died in an automobile accident, leaving three small children. My little brother was six months old, I was a year and a half, and my big sister was almost three. Dona and I are only seventeen months apart and during our growing-up years, we always shared a bedroom.

Many nights we went to bed afraid and lonely, and we were somewhat confused about life. Dona wasn't sheepish about her nighttime fears; I always tried to hide mine. Our bedroom was small and we had twin beds that were always next to each other, separated only by the walking distance between them. Frequently, well after we should have been asleep, Dona would whisper to me, "Are you awake?" I often pretended I hadn't heard her. If I answered her question, she would sometimes ask if she could climb into bed with me for a while. More often she just kept asking in a louder and more intense whisper, "Are you awake?" until I finally answered, or until she *did* wake me up!

My sister always wanted to talk, but after I became tired, she would settle for a slim amount of physical contact. She would whisper "pinkies" to me and I knew what that meant. We would reach across the narrow space between our beds, both lying on our tummies, and hook our pinkie fingers together and swing them to comfort each other. The touch of a sister's hand consoled both of us. Finally we would fall asleep peacefully.

I never realized how much our "pinkie swing" meant to me until she went away to college a year and a half ahead of me. Suddenly I was gripped with fear, finding myself in a bedroom at night all alone for the first time. I started pinning Scripture to my window shade and pulling it down to my eye level and reading it over and over again until sleep overtook me. "Thou wilt keep him in perfect peace, whose mind is stayed on thee" (Isaiah 26:3 KJV). "I will lie down and sleep in peace, for you alone, O Lord, make me dwell in safety" (Psalm 4:8). Those words made my heart calm and peaceful.

Dona and I are grown women now and both of us know that Scripture is the best antidote to fear. As adults, Dona and I occasionally have a chance to hang out together. We still face fearful situations. With a smile, one of us will call out "pinkie swing," and we instantly know the comfort and courage that comes from a supportive sister. God gave two little girls reassurance through "the nights of life." And he's still doing that today.

. . . .

So do not fear, for I am with you; do not be dismayed,
for I am your God. I will strengthen you and help you;
I will uphold you with my righteous right hand.

ISAIAH 41:10

two cooks and a skillet of noodles

Bonnie Afman Emmorey

. . . .

It is bad to suppress your laughter because when you do,
it goes back down and spreads to your hips.

FRED ALLEN

*B*eing the fourth daughter born in the Afman household had one big advantage. I never had to learn how to cook. If Mother was gone, one of my older sisters took over the meal preparation.

After our sisters Carol and Jennie left for college, Paula and I became the oldest of four children still living at home. Our mother soon realized there was a problem. Paula is just eighteen months older than I am, and she hadn't learned how to cook either. I was a junior in high school, and Paula was a freshman in college. By this time Mother didn't have much hope that a crash course in home economics would help us.

It was the seventies — long before there was a microwave oven in every kitchen. Mother kept a stash of pot pies in the freezer for us. If we came home and found ourselves on our own, we would just pop a pie in the oven and we had dinner.

One summer day Paula and I arrived home after working all day and no one else was there. No problem. I flipped on the switch to preheat the oven and left the room to change my clothes. Paula and I were back in the kitchen about a half hour later, ready to put in the pot pies — but we discovered a problem. Mom had left two pounds of ground beef in the oven to thaw.

We had a dilemma! The meat was already half-cooked, and we knew Mother wouldn't be happy if it was wasted, so we decided to make something out of it. We scrounged through the cupboards and found a box of Hamburger Helper. Surely, this box would solve our problem.

Paula got out the electric skillet and finished cooking the meat while I prepared to mix in the remaining ingredients. I was a little concerned because the mix called for one pound of meat and we had two, but Paula assured me that we could make it work.

Once everything was in the pan, we weren't too sure. Our concoction didn't look very appetizing. The box said we were making goulash, but there was way too much meat. We knew we'd have to add more ingredients. Paula suggested it needed more color, so she added a whole quart of Mother's canned tomatoes. I thought it needed more noodles to balance out all the tomatoes, so I found a box of elbow macaroni and dumped that into the mixture. We replaced the lid and prayed for a miracle.

A few minutes later, something odd happened. Our makeshift dinner was oozing out from under the lid and running down the side of the pan. When Paula lifted the cover, our creation poured out. The original mixture had *doubled* in size and was continuing to grow. The noodles were expanding — getting bigger and bigger! Our concoction was running off the stove and down on the floor. We were in trouble and we knew it.

At that moment Mother and Dad came in the door. Paula and I were trying not to fall on the slippery noodles that were now spreading out on the floor, and we were trying our best to keep some of our dinner in the pan. But it kept coming and coming. We soon realized our situation was out of control. Even Mother recognized the humor of the moment, and we stood there in the middle of those slimy noodles and laughed out loud. Here we were — two grown women — who couldn't even make Hamburger Helper!

It soon occurred to us that we hadn't read the directions. Who knew that noodles had to be *cooked* before they were added to the other ingredients? Even Mother couldn't save our creation. It was beyond hope! We tried giving it to the dog, but she turned her nose up at it. After cleaning up that awful mess, the whole family ended up eating pot pies.

Paula and I are both grown now, and we *did* eventually learn how to cook. However, we still break into a sweat when we see a box of Hamburger Helper. And we find ourselves laughing uncontrollably when we watch noodles expanding in hot water. We've also discovered that *following directions* is an important part of life.

* * *

Those who listen to instruction will prosper;
those who trust the Lord will be happy.

PROVERBS 16:20 NLT

trick or treat?

Lianne M. Belkas and Janis A. Wadden

· ·

*If you don't understand how a woman could both love her sister
dearly and want to wring her neck at the same time,
then you were probably an only child.*

LINDA SUNSHINE

*W*hen I was nine, my thirteen-year-old sister Janis became a teenager who thought it wasn't "cool" for her to be associating with a kid my age — especially when her friends were around. We often had sisterly spats and I was *never* allowed to touch her things or borrow her clothes.

One Halloween when I was in fourth grade, I found out a costume party had been scheduled for later that day. My heart sank. I knew my mother would be at work when I arrived home from school, so there was no way she could help me to throw a costume together. I would have to miss the party, and I wouldn't be with any of my friends. I moped all the way home — heartbroken.

When I finally sulked my way through the front door, my sister was hanging out in her room, listening to records with her best friend. They must have heard the door slam and my sister stuck her head out the door and saw me. There I was, a cloud of despair hanging over my head.

"Hey, Squirt, what's wrong?" she asked.

"Nothing," I moaned. "You wouldn't care anyway."

"No, really we *do*. Can we help?" By this time my sister and her friend had come out of the bedroom and were standing in front of me in the den. I related my tale of woe.

Confidently, Janis smiled and said, "We can fix that!" She put her arm around me and led me to her room, with her best friend following close behind.

My sister furrowed her brow and spoke aloud, more to herself than to anyone else, "Let's see; what would be a really cool costume?"

"I know," chimed in her friend. "How about a go-go dancer!"

"Yes! That's it!" They smiled in unison and congratulated each other. Then they started diving into the closets and jewelry cases.

My depressed mood was definitely lifting, but I was still apprehensive. In a strange sense I felt like Cinderella who was about to be transformed into a princess by none other than the wicked stepsisters. Was this for real, or were they planning some sort of a trick? Why were they being nice to me?

They turned in my direction with their hands full of creative treasures.

"Here, put this on," Janis ordered as she tossed an orange and brown striped knit minidress at me.

"And put these on," her friend added as she handed me a pair of white plastic knee-high go-go boots, complete with high heels.

When I was finally dressed, they completed my ensemble by wrapping my waist with a gold hoop-ringed belt and loading my arms and neck with multiple bangle bracelets and beads. Then came the finishing touch — makeup! They carefully applied cheek color, eye shadow, and lipstick to my beaming face.

"Voila!" they shouted. "You look *great*! Now get out of here and have a good time."

Janis smiled as she nudged me toward the door. I turned and gave both of them big hugs and smiles. By this time my tears of gratitude were threatening to ruin their exquisite makeup job. As I walked to the party, my jewelry jingled and jangled the whole way. I felt beautiful and my heart was singing.

Looking back, I don't remember much about the party. I don't even think I had a very good time. But I will always remember the day my sister revealed her true heart and demonstrated her love for me. It was the best Halloween day of my life!

* * *

Therefore, as God's chosen people, holy and dearly loved,
clothe yourselves with compassion, kindness, humility,
gentleness and patience.

COLOSSIANS 3:12

the throne room

Carol Kent

. . . .

Sisters and friends are God's life preservers.

ANONYMOUS

*M*y best childhood memories are from the year we moved into the big old farmhouse at the end of Foreman Road. The main road dead-ended at the edge of our property line, and very few people ventured down this country lane without an invitation. It would have been a lonely time in my life, except for one key fact — I already had three sisters (one more would be born later, but we didn't know about her yet). And nobody could feel alone for long with that many girls in the house.

The farmhouse had a big old space heater in the living room, and that room was connected to the kitchen, the music room, the master bedroom, the bathroom, and the steps that led to the sisters' quarters upstairs. The house was the commanding cornerstone for thirty-five acres of farmland, but it had one main flaw. In spite of numerous bedrooms, there was only *one* bathroom in that gigantic old house. That room defied the norm for the period in which it was built because it was a *big* bathroom, complete with an old-fashioned shower. All of my sisters enjoyed taking their turn at standing in the robust stream of water that cascaded from the antiquated showerhead.

Near the shower was the commode — and with so many people in our family, it was often in use. Our mother referred to this popular appliance as "the throne," and often one would hear a voice outside the door saying, "Is anybody sitting on the throne now? I need to get in there!" Very quickly that room was dubbed "The Throne Room."

That room also contained the best mirror in the house for squeezing pimples and putting on makeup, so it was not uncommon to have one sister in the shower, one at the mirror, another with her head propped up on a pillow on the floor in front of the hamper, and another sitting on the "throne," with or without the lid down. Some of my most memorable talks with my sisters took place in that wonderful confined space where all pretense was gone and honest repartee, mindless bantering, and humorous jousting took place on a regular basis. We discussed "coming of age," boys, church, clothes, and beauty tips. Often, the wrinkled skin on the sister who did her talking through the shower curtain was a reminder that we had all been in that room too long.

My sisters are grown now, but some things in life don't change much. Last weekend my husband and I were visiting our granddaughters in Florida. It was the night before we were to leave to catch an early plane home. I was in the bathroom removing my makeup and soon realized I wasn't alone. Seven-year-old Hannah had slipped into the empty bathtub fully clothed and settled in for some conversation. Chelsea, age ten, positioned herself near the towel rack. My daughter-in-love April soon claimed "the throne" (lid down), and very soon our conversation was animated.

Glancing over at Hannah, I noticed numerous unclothed Barbie dolls in the wire rack attached to the bathtub. With a chuckle I looked at the girls and said, "What's the deal with all of these naked dolls in the tub?"

Hannah immediately picked up one of the dolls and said, "This is Olympic Barbie and she's teaching the rest of the girls how to swim, but we didn't want to get their clothes wet so we took them off." My granddaughter hit a button on the back of the doll and sure enough, Olympic Barbie began to do the breaststroke. "She even has a gold medal," Hannah added. We all laughed as they demonstrated the swimming lessons.

My eyes soon landed on the only male doll in the group. Poor Ken was missing both legs. Evidently Olympic Barbie had worn the guy out with her advanced swimming techniques. The girls giggled as their mommy picked up the physically impaired Ken and used her own fingers to make new appendages for him. Quite unexpectedly he was leaping and running and even looked somewhat normal. Laughter again filled the room.

Suddenly there was a moment of silence and Hannah piped up with, "Grammy, why can't you stay longer? Why do you have to leave us tomorrow? We don't want you to go yet."

A warm, familiar emotion engulfed me as I looked around that room at two little sisters, their mom, and me — Grammy Carol. I realized that girls seem to talk best in the confined quarters of "the throne room." It felt good. It felt right.

Love one another deeply, from the heart.

1 PETER 1:22

sister squad to the rescue

Pam Cronk

*There is a special bond and a unique strength
shared between sisters.*

ANONYMOUS

*J*t was a cloudless, sunny, warm morning in June
2001. The phone rang. I picked up the receiver and
my brother-in-law said, "Hi. This is Mike. Our house
burned this morning." He spoke stoically. After telling us that
nobody was hurt, he explained some of the details. Then he
said, "Here, I'll let you talk to your sister Lois."

An emotional conversation ensued, with Mom joining in
on our other phone. We learned that although the house was
still standing, the contents were all burned, melted, or charred.
Stunned and in tears, Mom and I told Lois that we would pray
and we would let the rest of the family know what happened.

As I hung up the phone, one of Lois's comments lingered
in my mind: "We're watching the firemen try to save some of
our memories, but nothing really matters except our family's

safety and our relationship with the Lord. We know God is in control and has a reason for this."

I called my other two sisters. The following day we worked out the details of jobs and family that would free us to travel from our home in Michigan to Wisconsin to comfort and help our sister and her family during this crisis. At the time, we were not fully aware of what we were facing. So equipped with industrial strength dust-and-particle masks, gloves, work clothes, a laptop, and as much cheer as we could muster, we prayerfully left on our 400-plus-mile road trip.

We spent our travel time reminiscing about many "sister weekends," knowing that what lay ahead would be a totally different kind of reunion. Still, we hoped to bring in some of the heartwarming fun and craziness we always experienced when we had sister-time together. The three of us created some makeshift badges to wear that would serve as smile-makers when we arrived in Wausau for the big cleanup operation. They read: "SEARCH, SNIFF, SCRATCH, SWEEP . . . SISTER SQUAD TO THE RESCUE!"

As we drove up to their home, we saw our sister Lois and our brother-in-law, Mike, dressed in borrowed clothes, working in the garage with Mike's sister. Lois squealed as she saw the car and came to greet us. We got out of the car and charged up the driveway with our masks, gloves, and badges on. Our appearance did bring laughter, along with tears. We enjoyed a group hug and then got to work.

Our job was to sort through items that could be restored and categorize them on inventory sheets. It was over 95 degrees outside and much hotter in the charred, stench-filled shell that had been our sister's lovely home. As we worked, we made jokes when we found items all of us remembered. Periodically Lois said, "I am so glad to have my sisters here with me. You have come to my rescue!"

As that first exhausting day came to a close, we decided Lois should stay with us at the hotel. When she arrived, she was carrying a borrowed child-sized floral suitcase, and we all burst into laughter. "I'm going to Grandma's!" Lois exclaimed, chuckling. We spent the rest of the evening in the pool getting some needed hydrotherapy.

The rest of that week, four wiped-out sisters reminisced, cried, prayed, made inventories of household goods, wiped soot off ourselves, watched dumpsters being packed and hauled away, and investigated new possibilities for furniture and other necessary items. We talked on the phone with out-of-town family members, snuggled, ate meals with gracious friends and neighbors, enjoyed chocolate from our traditional "Sisters' Chocolate Smorgasbord," completed a hard copy of the insurance inventory, and bonded more closely than ever before.

We realized, along with Mike and Lois, that material things aren't the important things in life. It's the loving relationships God has given us with himself and with our family. Our Sister

Rescue Squad was a reminder that in good times and bad times sisters need each other.

. . . .

And we know that in all things God works for the good of those who love him, who have been called according to his purpose.

Romans 8:28

my sister kicked me!

Sonia Kohler

. . . .

The more impossible the situation,
the greater God accomplishes His work.

CHARLES SWINDOLL

*I*t was a crisp sunny fall afternoon, and my son and daughter had just come home from school. They hurried outside to play soccer. We had only moved to this new community six weeks earlier. The transition had been difficult, and I was encouraged to see the children playing outside with a new friend.

All my pleasant thoughts were shattered when moments later my eight-year-old son, John, ran in the front door crying in what appeared to be severe pain. Within a couple moments he was rolling on the living room floor screaming, saying, "My sister kicked me!" He was pointing to the side of his abdomen, but he also complained that he felt a shooting pain in his shoulder. Not too much later he was throwing up blood, and I knew his condition was extremely serious. It didn't seem like a normal reaction after an accidental kick while playing soccer.

I made a couple of frantic phone calls, then drove John to a nearby emergency room. On the ride there he seemed only partially conscious; he was in intense pain. When we registered and were asked what happened, John again said, "My sister kicked me." He was examined by a doctor and sent for a CT scan. Whenever he was asked what happened, his response was the same: "My sister kicked me." Everyone said, "Oh, your *sister* did this?" with a note of surprise, as if they expected to hear that his sister had a black belt in karate.

The early diagnosis was a possible ruptured spleen or a severe kidney injury. John was transferred by ambulance to another hospital late that night. Both the ambulance driver and the paramedic asked John what happened, and his reply sounded like a broken record: "My sister kicked me." I made a call home, updating the family on John's condition. I spoke with his petite twelve-year-old sister, the originator of the perilous kick. Laura was crying, very upset to have caused such a severe injury to her brother. She was extremely apologetic, and I told her the best thing she could do was to pray for John.

After a sleepless and prayerful night in the pediatric intensive care ward, more tests were ordered, and my husband and I had a series of consultations with numerous doctors. That day is still a blur in my mind. Finally, we met with a pediatric surgeon who explained that an experienced radiologist had looked at John's CT scan and found something significant. They suspected the real problem was a very large tumor, which had ruptured inside John's kidney.

The information they shared next was the most troubling because the descriptions of various tumor possibilities all contained the "C" word — cancer. I was in shock. How could my child possibly have cancer? John had a biopsy, and we prayed for a conclusive answer. Each doctor asked him how he felt and how this happened to him and he repeatedly responded, "My sister kicked me."

When the results of the biopsy came back, we were told John had a rapidly growing cancerous tumor of the kidney, called a Wilm's tumor. Even though there are only about 350 cases in the nation per year, this type of cancer is considered one of the most treatable childhood cancers — if detected early. There are very few methods for detecting this tumor until it gets so large that the child's abdomen is protruding. The only other method of detection is accidental trauma.

Soon we heard the doctors tell John, "It's a good thing your sister kicked you."

Laura realized the value of what she had accidentally done. During dinner at the hospital one evening, Laura gave my husband a high five as she said, "So, it was a *good* thing I kicked John!"

Most parents don't condone kicking as a desirable behavior, but this kick was delivered exactly to the spot where it needed to go. Laura kicked the cancerous kidney with just enough force to let us know the tumor was present. We discovered later that this large tumor was contained within the kidney and had not spread to any other vital organs.

After nearly a year of treatment that included chemotherapy, radiation, and removal of his kidney, John is considered in remission with little chance for recurrence of the original cancer. He is an energetic, happy, and healthy young man.

John now says, "My sister kicked me, and that kick saved my life."

Sometimes life's unexpected "kicks" are a much-needed wake-up call.

. . . .

It is the Lord who goes before you. He will be with you; he will not fail you or forsake you. Do not fear or be dismayed.

DEUTERONOMY 31:8 NRSV

blessed assurance
in the hayloft

Carol Kent

. . . .

*There is some unwritten rule between sisters that you are there for
each other, no matter what the situation.*

LORI SHANKLE

*J*f walls could talk, the farmhouse and barn at the end
of Foreman Road could fill a book. The house sat
high on a hill, and the yard gently sloped down to a
picturesque rippling creek that flowed through many of the
thirty-five acres that made up the farm. On the other side of the
house stood a tall weeping willow tree that graced the yard with
a fairy-tale charm. Just beyond the big circle driveway stood the
barn. Dad wasn't a farmer, but he rented space in that aging
structure to neighbors, who filled the lofts with bales of hay.

That hayloft provided endless hours of fun for me and my
sisters. Our adventuresome cousin Ronnie would stack the
bales of hay to create a maze of hidden passageways where we

could hide without being discovered. When other children visited, we would busy ourselves for hours and never tire of the fun that could be found in that old dilapidated barn.

I often sought the solitude of the barn when life got hectic, and the hayloft was a favorite place for me to read. Just enough sunshine came through the slats that I could get some very good light high in the loft area. It became my place of solitude for spending time alone with God.

One day as I was having my quiet time in the hayloft, I heard the sound of footsteps. My sister Jennie had found my favorite place. The look on her face told me something was wrong. Although four years separated us in age, there was a tender closeness in our relationship. Jennie had rheumatic fever that required long rest periods, and she often grew weary of the time she had to spend in bed.

"What's wrong, Jennie?"

My little sister paused a moment and then blurted out her secret: "Carol, one afternoon when I was five years old I didn't want to go back to bed. I knew Mama would listen to me for a long time if I talked about the Lord, and that night I asked her about what it meant to be a real Christian. She took lots of time and told me that Jesus paid the price for my sins when he died on the cross and that he rose from the dead. She asked me if I wanted to be born into God's family and I told her I did. I asked lots more questions, and finally Mama prayed with me, and I asked Jesus to come into my heart."

Jennie was crying by this time. I tried to be encouraging. "That's a good thing, Jen. You became a Christian that day. Why are you crying?"

With agonizing sobs, my almost eight-year-old sister confessed, "The afternoon I prayed with Mama I didn't want to go back to bed, and I think I'm probably not really a Christian, and I'm probably going to hell because I think I just prayed that prayer with her so I could stay up later."

Guilt is a cruel companion, and my tenderhearted sister had finally revealed her deepest fear. Seeing me in the hayloft reading my Bible had triggered her confession.

At twelve years of age I felt an enormous responsibility and a joy-filled opportunity as I slipped an arm around my sister. "Jennie, if you're not positive that you're a Christian, let's pray right now. You can pray that prayer again, and if you didn't really mean it the first time, you can know *for sure* that you've been born into God's family today."

That afternoon two sisters got down on their knees side by side next to a bale of hay, and Jennie sweetly confessed her sin to God and asked Jesus to be her Savior. As we stood up, her face was beaming and the assurance of her faith had replaced a guilty conscience. Jennie had become a "for real" Christian.

For the wages of sin is death, but the gift of God is eternal life in Christ Jesus our Lord.

ROMANS 6:23

my hair-brained extreme makeover

Brenda Fassett

....

Big sisters are the crabgrass in the lawn of life.

CHARLES M. SCHULTZ

The summer I turned eight started out normal enough. My sister Sheila, seven, and I had finished our school year at the end of May. We were giddy with the prospect of long days of play and high adventure. The fact that I had an early June birthday was the icing on the cake. Cake indeed! And ice cream! And presents! Within days, my aunt Charlotte arrived with a small swimming pool in tow. We knew life didn't get any better than this. But after a few days of swimming and splashing, we began to get an itch to do other things — like playing with our "old faithful" toys.

Sheila and I pulled out our tried-and-true Barbie and Midge dolls. We each had one doll. Midge was my favorite. She had beautiful long auburn hair styled in a permanent pageboy. Sheila had a classic blonde ponytail Barbie.

Then I came up with a brilliant idea, sort of an *extreme* makeover! I was so excited I could barely speak.

"Sheil," I squealed, "let's make Barbie wigs!"

"Barbie wigs? What do you mean?" she asked.

"Let's make wigs for our Barbies so they can have new hairdos. It'll be great!"

"How do you make Barbie wigs, Brenny?"

"It's easy. You take some hair and put it on the doll's head, okay?" I was about to burst with excitement!

"Where do we get the hair from, Bren?" my little sister asked innocently.

"Well, I guess we'll have to use yours," I answered.

Sheila's eyes flew open, and her face turned white. "*My* hair? Why *my* hair? Why not *your* hair?" she demanded.

"Well, we *can* use my hair, but do you know how to cut hair for wigs? I've got a pretty good idea how to do it. Do *you*?"

Her shoulders slumped. She knew my advanced age and superior skills had her beat.

"How much hair?" she asked as she stroked her shoulder-length hair.

"Not much," I replied.

"Mom will know," she said matter-of-factly.

"I'll just take a little from the back. She won't notice."

"You really, *really* know how to make Barbie wigs, Brenny?"

"Yes," I said, lying unashamedly.

I got the scissors and went to work. I cut. And I cut. And I cut some more.

Before long there was *a lot* of hair on the floor. It wasn't hanging in nice straight sections like Sheila's haircut anymore. It was just a pile of hair. A big, messy mishmash pile of hair. A no-rhyme-or-reason pile of hair.

Then I looked at Sheila's head. I was aghast! Most of the hair from the back of her head was gone! How had I cut it so short? How had I cut so *much*? Suddenly, an overwhelming truth began to surge through my brain — *this was a really, really, really bad idea!*

Sheila turned around and looked down at all her hair on the floor. With the hopeful eyes of a trusting little sister, she held up a fistful of her hair. "So, how do we make it into wigs, Brenny?"

That moment is forever emblazed in my mind. I had let my sister down before, but this was the first time I had blown it in such a big way. How would I answer her question?

"I don't know," I admitted.

"What do you mean you don't know? You said you *knew* how!" she cried.

"I thought I did."

"You *said* you *did!*"

"I thought I did."

Sheila felt the back of her head and started to cry. I didn't have enough sense to cry. But I had a plan. I convinced my sister that if she stayed in the swimming pool all day, Mom wouldn't notice her hair because it would be wet. Sheila ran for the pool, where she submerged her head and stayed wet for the remainder of the afternoon.

At suppertime, a waterlogged Sheila was ordered out of the pool. Mom saw her hair. We confessed to the crime and were given our sentence. Sheila would have to have a very short haircut to "fix" the mess I had made, and I, as the originator of the idea, would receive the same haircut. And so it was that the two oldest sisters both had fashionable "pixies" for the summer of 1965.

I meekly asked Sheila to forgive me for talking her into such a bad idea. She put her arm around me and said, "It's okay, Brenny. It will be fun to have the same haircut this summer."

That wasn't the last wild idea I dreamed up, but over time, I learned the art of "looking before leaping." I also learned that if you're going to plan a "hair-brained" scheme, there's no better person to bring along for the ride than your sister.

* * *

Be kind and compassionate to one another, forgiving each other, just as in Christ God forgave you.

EPHESIANS 4:32

a tribute to "foo foo"

Carol Kent

* *

To get the full value of joy, you must have someone to divide it with.

MARK TWAIN

*M*y sister Paula Sue came out of the womb with big bright eyes, fine silky hair, a perfect complexion, pink tulip-shaped lips, and an ability to bring sunshine into any situation. As the baby became an adolescent, and puberty evolved her into a grown woman, heads turned when she entered a room. When Paula grew up, her smile could make a ship full of sailors jump overboard in hopes of being rescued by this beauty.

You might think that the above description would bring envy to a family with five girls, but that wasn't the case. Certain people are born to bring optimism, hope, and joy to this world, and Paula is one of those people. Our pet name for Paula is "Foo Foo," which to her sisters means: "This girl was born for celebration and spontaneity!"

A short while ago, I wrote a list of the things I appreciate most about her.

To My Pretty Foo Foo,

- You always make me feel loved.
- When I call, you don't act like I've interrupted your day and you have "things to do" that are more important than my problems.
- You dress in a funky, delightfully flamboyant way that makes heads turn when you enter a room.
- You have big hair, glamorous makeup, sparkling jewelry, high energy, and exciting ideas for outrageous getaways.
- You make everyone in the room with you feel important.
- You are never embarrassed to do wacky things.
- You are still young enough at heart to play "dress up."
- You have become "Auntie Foo Foo" to your nieces and nephews, and they know when you arrive, fun and celebration are walking into the room too.
- You would give your last dime to help a sister in need.
- You have demonstrated how to survive the loss of a marriage, the devastation of betrayal, and the death of a dream — and you have successfully climbed out of the "stuff" of life to show me how to smile again, even when life is hard.

Biologically speaking, we can't pick our sisters. However, when you get a good one — you know it. My pretty "Foo Foo" was custom designed by God to be in my family because he knew how much I would need the sunshine of her smile.

. . . .

A good woman is hard to find, and worth far more than diamonds.... Her clothes are well-made and elegant, and she always faces tomorrow with a smile. When she speaks she has something worthwhile to say, and she always says it kindly.

PROVERBS 31:10, 25–26 MSG

what would *you* like, sis?

Lucinda Secrest McDowell

....

The best things in life aren't things.

ANONYMOUS

*I*f y'all don't want the silver tea service, I'd love to have it," I said to my two sisters as we surveyed our parents' vast living and dining rooms.

"No problem, Cindy, and I could really use the bronze fireplace fixtures," Susan replied.

"That's great because I'd love to give Catharine this dining room set for her little family if y'all agree," Cathy pointed out.

And so it went—three adult sisters from three different parts of the country meeting to divide our parents' home furnishings. A month earlier Mama and Daddy had moved to a small apartment in a nearby retirement community. They had lovingly furnished it with their favorite things. But it couldn't hold everything collected during fifty-five years of marriage, so they invited us to divide up the rest for ourselves and for our children.

What a daunting task! We had all heard horror stories of siblings fighting over who got what, but here we were making decisions amicably. *Sisters* were obviously greater than *stuff*! Whenever two or more of us wanted the same thing, we simply drew straws or rotated the picking process.

I'm not saying it wasn't hard. We had to make quick decisions, and the magnitude of the task threatened to overwhelm us. But even in the emotional stress of dismantling our family home, we each remembered what our parents had taught us well — *people are more important than things.*

As we sorted through the house, we were each drawn to certain objects because of sentimental attachment or a fond memory associated with them. Not once did anyone say, "How much is this worth?" These items were precious to us because they were an extension of our parents and their legacy of love.

It took us a full week, and though we got tired and even frustrated, we never argued over one single thing. In fact, the process drew us even closer together as sisters since we reminisced the whole time. I consider that to be an extraordinary tribute to our parents' raising us with godly priorities.

Today our respective homes in Connecticut, Oklahoma, and Georgia are each made cozier by the objects we chose and will pass down to our children. And Mama and Daddy can enjoy them whenever they visit.

....

Do not store up for yourselves treasures on earth, where moth and rust destroy, and where thieves break in and steal. But store up for yourselves treasures in heaven, where moth and rust do not destroy, and where thieves do not break in and steal. For where your treasure is, there your heart will be also.

MATTHEW 6:19–21

bubbles and troubles

Bonnie Afman Emmorey

....

Bubble, bubble, toil and trouble.

SHAKESPEARE, *MACBETH*

On Saturday in the Afman household there were two things we could always count on: first, we would spend the day cleaning; second, we would be in line for the bathtub scrub. In case you're wondering, that wasn't the only day we bathed, but it was mandatory on Saturday night. Come Sunday morning, there would be a row of shiny clean faces in the Afman pew at church. (With six children in our family, we took up a whole pew.)

Our Dutch heritage was most evident on those Saturdays. As the old saying goes, "Cleanliness is next to godliness," and at our home that meant house *and body*! Since my sister Paula was the closest in age to me, we often bathed together in those early years. We had such fun, splashing and laughing in that oversized old-fashioned tub. It was well worth all the work that came first.

At the time of "the bubble incident," Paula was seven years old and I was six. Our turn for the bathtub came and, with it, a wonderfully creative idea was born. We decided to take our mother's dish soap, add it to our bath water, and make a wonderful foamy bathing extravaganza. Our idea worked to perfection. We poured almost the whole bottle of soap into the water, jumped in, and stood side by side facing the long slope of that big, comfortable old bathtub. We leaned forward, placed our hands at the top of the slope to give us balance, and started to run in place. Using our unlimited supply of youthful energy, we churned and agitated the water, and the soapy bubbles started to billow and foam.

Before long we had a beautiful mass of bubbles towering over the top edge of that tub. We laughed jubilantly and played to our hearts' content. Paula and I created high, bouffant hairstyles. We gave ourselves voluptuous, womanly bubble figures. We played in the tub of bubbles until our fingers and toes were as shriveled as prunes.

Unfortunately, we had not thought ahead. We let out all the water and, to our amazement, the bubbles stayed behind. *Bubble, bubble, toil and trouble,* indeed! Draining the water out of the tub seemed to have no impact on the high volume of bubbles. We had just as many bubbles *without* the water. In fact, in our young minds, it seemed that they were still *growing.* We began to panic. Our mother was not going to be happy that we had wasted most of her dish soap; we were picturing major trouble in our immediate future.

We *had* to get rid of those bubbles. Paula and I had created them with such delight and enjoyment. We needed to get rid of them with the same intensity. We tried flushing them by adding water. That was a mistake! It only created more bubbles and more trouble. We tried clapping them. Too slow. We knew we'd be working on this mission way past our bedtime — and we'd be caught. But when you put two Afman girls together, they can solve almost anything.

Paula and I moved into action. We discovered that it was possible to crush and dissolve the bubbles by taking our wash-cloths and smothering them. It was a long, laborious job. We were exhausted from our hard work. But we continued until every bubble was gone. Down the drain. Crushed into oblivion. Our troubles were over! We got away with it! Our mother was not going to find out after all.

More than forty years have passed since that bathtub event, yet the memory is still vivid. This past Christmas, Paula, Mother, and I were together while vacationing in Florida and the bubble incident was revisited. With much laughter, Paula and I *finally* admitted to Mother what we had done. Mother laughed right along with us, assuring us that she never knew about the "bubble extravaganza," and she never missed the soap.

Even though Paula and I now live almost a continent apart, we still share our bubbles and troubles regularly. When we're together, the laughter bubbles out of us, and our troubles seem to float away. When we're apart, cell phones and the Internet keep us connected. Participating in ongoing sister escapades gives us great joy. We have bubbled with trouble in the past and I'm sure we will bubble with trouble in the future, but I have every confidence that, together, we will work hard to dissolve our disasters and multiply our joys. Life's problems are always easier to handle with a sister at your side.

* *

Friends love through all kinds of weather,
and families stick together in all kinds of trouble.

PROVERBS 17:17 MSG

a picture is worth
a thousand words

Barbara Bond-Howard

....

*You don't make a photograph just with a camera. You bring to the
act of photography all the pictures you have seen, the books you
have read, the music you have heard and the people you have loved.*

ANSEL ADAMS

*M*ost people can easily recall what they were doing on September 11, 2001. But do you remember September 10, 2001? I remember it well. My sister, Jeanie, had flown from Green Bay, Wisconsin, to my home in Washington State after our dad died. We had claimed his ashes a few days earlier, and we were spending time together.

On September 10, we decided to have a "sisters picture" taken. We went shopping to find matching shirts to go with our already matching Venetian crosses. But we had a problem. Everything that looked good on her didn't look good on me.

The clothes I liked, she didn't. Jeanie wanted to keep shopping for clothes, and I just wanted to go to a bookstore and bury myself in some good reading.

"Barbie," she said, using my childhood name, "this is so much fun!" I brushed it off. It *wasn't* fun. Dad had died, his remains were in my car, and I was supposed to find a shirt that was flattering so we could have our (*gasp*) picture taken?

My usually optimistic nature was not kicking in. I was sad. I didn't want a new shirt. I didn't want to be in a mall. And I certainly didn't want my picture taken. I wanted my dad back. We finally agreed on matching shirts, and we got our picture taken. While the photos were being processed, we had lunch together, knowing that our "sister time" was quickly coming to a close. When the pictures were ready, we returned to my home so she could begin packing.

Today our mom has this picture proudly framed in her study. Jeanie has her copy prominently placed in her family room. My duplicate picture is stuffed in a desk drawer because I don't want to be reminded of how sad I felt that day. Jeanie looks pretty good in the photo, and I look . . . well, I look *depressed*.

My sister was scheduled to fly home the next day, but we woke up to the tragedy of the World Trade Center disaster and to the horrifying news of the other terrorist attacks. We soon learned Jeanie wouldn't be taking any flights that day. We were devastated by the events of September 11, and we were still mourning our father's death. If I thought my September 10 photo looked depressing, I am glad there were no photos taken of me on September 11.

It was four days before Jeanie was able to leave for her home via train. During our unexpected time together we drove up to Mount Baker Lake in the Cascade Mountains and took a ferry ride through Puget Sound. All the while we continued sharing memories of Dad and of his influence on our lives. Then I suddenly remembered his remains were still in the backseat of my car!

With a chuckle, Jeanie and I realized Dad would have loved being with his two daughters as they talked, walked, laughed, and cried during our unforeseen extra time together. We realized his unexpected "presence" in the backseat of the car was not an accident. It helped to make our unplanned "sister time" a sacred and precious memory. It's a mental photograph I will never forget.

. . . .

I will exalt you, O Lord, for you lifted me out of the depths . . .
weeping may remain for a night,
but rejoicing comes in the morning.

PSALM 30:1, 5

the sister with five mothers

Joy Carlson

● ●

*Enjoy the little things, for one day you may look back
and realize they were the big things.*

ROBERT BRAULT

*M*y birth was a complete shock to my family. I have sometimes been referred to as "the surprise that wasn't menopause." At age forty-two my mother gave birth to her sixth child and her fifth daughter, which meant I instantly had four older sisters. In truth, it felt more like I had my "real" mom and four additional mothers.

To my surprise, I was never made to feel like an inconvenience. I may have stolen Dad's heart and undoubtedly Mother's lap, but if my sisters ever resented me, they made sure it wasn't obvious. My sisters taught me to enjoy *the little things* in life — and now I realize they were *the big things.*

Mother #1: My "real" mother is a storyteller and has reminded me by example that many of life's greatest lessons will be learned by my children more easily if they are wrapped in an unforgettable story.

Mother #2: Carol is my oldest sister and she gave me my first nephew. She reinforced the value of the "little gifts and letters" that I often sent to her son, letting me know that those small acts of kindness produced great encouragement and motivation.

Mother #3: Jennie came next and she was my "artsy" sister. She brought home fascinating projects from school and took the time to teach me how to make child-sized versions of her wonderful creations. From Jennie I learned how to think outside the box.

Mother #4: Paula (or "Paulie" as I used to call her) spoiled me, and it was wonderful. She was also my Sunday school teacher. For the Christmas program one year, she wanted her class to look their best, so with her own money, she bought green turtlenecks for all the boys and made red velveteen skirts for the girls. I don't know if we all recited our parts perfectly, but we looked outstanding. Paula taught me that generosity makes people feel valued and significant.

Mother #5: Bonnie was closest to me in age — but still nine years my senior. She had the amazing ability to create something out of virtually nothing. If I couldn't find anything to wear, she was the one who came up with a great outfit from my tired, worn-out separates. If a dress pattern called for three yards of fabric, she could make it look even better out of two. Bonnie taught me how to be creative on a shoestring budget.

Each of my sisters contributed greatly to who I am today as each mothered me in her own unique way. Today I have seven children of my own, and I'm grateful for learning early that the little things in life are the most important. Carol is the epitome of inspiration and encouragement. Jennie now spends time with my own children with the excess (and love) of a grandmother. Paula showed me how to generously invest in what is precious to me. Bonnie gave me vision, determination, and resourcefulness.

Our relationships have now matured into something more typical of sisters. But I've always had a hard time understanding how some unexpected babies arriving later in their parents' lives grow up feeling unwanted. But then, probably none of them had four big sisters and five wonderful mothers!

. . . .

Now to him who is able to do immeasurably more than all we ask or imagine, . . . to him be glory.

EPHESIANS 3:20–21

the most prized possession

Bonnie Afman Emmorey

∙∙

What I spent I lost; what I possessed is left to others;
what I gave away remains with me.

JOSEPH ADDISON

*D*uring our growing-up years we were actually
quite poor — not in the important matters of
life, just financially. We were rich in things that
really counted, such as love, generosity, and family traditions.

Some traditions were already established by the time I, the
fourth sister in the family, arrived. Early on, our creative mother
had instituted a wonderful Christmas gift-giving plan. Some
years we didn't have money to spend on gifts for each other, so
she encouraged each of us to take our most prized possession
and give it to the next sister in line.

Carol, the oldest, was the proud owner of the most beautiful white rabbit fur muff. In the winter, she brought it out every
Sunday and wore it with delight to church. Each one of us took
turns petting the beautiful fur when it came within our reach. It

was definitely her most prized possession, so that year Carol lovingly wrapped it and put it under the tree for our sister Jennie.

How Jennie loved and enjoyed that muff! It was her favorite gift and she looked forward to Sundays just to have the pleasure of wearing it. It was only in service during cold weather, and when summer came, the muff was carefully stored.

When summer finally came to an end and the first brisk day dawned, out came the muff and the enjoyment with it. Paula and I would vie to sit next to Jennie for the mere pleasure of petting the furry muff as often as possible. That year when Christmas arrived, Jennie, too, carefully wrapped the muff in holiday trimmings and labeled the gift to the next sister.

Oh, how delighted Paula was when she opened the much-loved, and now a bit worn, white fur muff. Somehow it became even more precious as time passed. I could hardly wait for the next Christmas, because I was almost certain to be next in line for the special gift.

Paula did not disappoint me and I finally had *my* turn at owning the beautiful white fur muff. It still had the string to go around the neck and felt warm when I tucked my hands inside. The small tear in the lining didn't lessen my enjoyment or pride in being the official owner of the muff.

My year passed far too quickly, and before I knew it, Christmas was right around the corner again. I *knew* the muff was my most prized possession, but the thought of giving it up troubled me. Since I didn't have a younger sister at that time (baby Joy was born nine years after my birth), and Carol and Jennie were getting older and losing their intense interest in the muff, I knew it should go back to Paula — but it was *so* hard. I wrapped the gift, put her name on the tag, and put it under the tree. But it was *too* difficult. I secretly retrieved the gift and unwrapped it. I lovingly caressed the now worn fur. It was still so beautiful to my young eyes.

But I knew better. I *had* to give it up! It was my greatest treasure, and it must be given to my sister. I had enjoyed it for a whole year, and my time of ownership had passed. I again wrapped the muff and put a new tag on it with Paula's name in bold letters. Once again I placed it with care under the tree.

I wish I could tell you how much pleasure Paula had opening her present and seeing the treasured muff. But I can't. You see, on Christmas Eve, I retrieved the muff and decided I couldn't give it up after all. I can't remember what I finally wrapped and *passed off* as a treasure, just so I could keep the muff. Not one of my sisters ever said a word to me about my selfishness, and I don't think they looked down on me for not passing it along — but I knew in my heart it was wrong.

Years later, Paula had a Christmas wedding, and each of the sisters wore red velvet dresses and, instead of flowers, we each carried beautiful white fur muffs. They reminded all of us of past Christmases when we gave each other things we cherished most, and they gave us a new memory to treasure in the future.

Without a doubt, my sisters demonstrated the meaning of true generosity during my growing-up years. I hope my behavior *today* lives up to their example. And if any of them ever needs a kidney, I'll be the first in line to be the donor. After all, I *did* keep the muff!

. . . .

All goes well for those who are generous.

Psalm 112:5 NLT

a changed heart

Jolanta Hoffmann

· ·

Chance made us sisters; hearts made us friends.

ANONYMOUS

*H*ow would you like a new sister?" my mom asked one night. "Your dad and I have decided to let Carlisa move in with us for her senior year of high school and to help her go to college."

Carlisa and I were not strangers. We had known each other for several years since she and her four siblings had begun coming to our downtown church through a bus ministry, which picked up kids from the housing projects. All five of them were musically talented, and we had sung together in choirs and music ensembles. My family had also helped them move from time to time. Carlisa and her sister even stayed with us for a few weeks after their mother tried to end her life. But I wasn't at all sure about having her become my new "sister." As a self-absorbed sixteen-year-old and the baby of the family, I wasn't eager to alter my status as the only child left at home.

Even though I was apprehensive, I could tell this was some-thing my kindhearted mom really felt God wanted us to do. So I smiled and said, "Sure, that's a great idea."

Carlisa moved her few belongings to the extra bedroom, and we started making our transition from friends to sisters. It wasn't so horrible having her around. I enjoyed having some-one to help me with my cleaning chores and to keep me com-pany when my mom and dad went out for the evening.

One day as I walked in the kitchen after school I heard Carlisa say, "Mom, can you help me with my math homework?"

Then I heard, "Wait until Dad gets home. He's better with math."

I left before either of them noticed me. *Did she say* Mom *and* Dad? *They aren't her mom and dad. They're mine!* I was very resentful every time I heard Carlisa refer to my parents in the very personal way I addressed them. But I didn't let anyone know how I felt.

As the year passed, Carlisa and I had more time being alone together. She began to open up. One day she said, "I like hav-ing a dad. My dad left the country when I was very young, and I don't remember him."

I felt embarrassed for not wanting her to call my father "Dad." My earlier apprehensions were melting into compas-sion. As we began talking about our early childhood, Carlisa told a story that knocked all of the resentment out of me.

"You're lucky to have such a great mom you can depend on. When I was seven years old, I had to live in the county parental home because my mom tried to commit suicide. My mother told me she would come back soon. I remember waiting on the bench outside every evening while the other kids were playing — looking for her to come back. She never did. I had to go to a foster home until she got back on her feet."

I was speechless. What kind of response could I give to *that*? I had been acting so selfish. I soon realized there was room for another sister in my life and heart. I could share my mom and dad with someone who had been through so much and had such a great need for security.

I hated to see that year end and have my new sister go away to college. But we weren't through being sisters, even though we no longer lived under the same roof. As the years passed, I celebrated when Carlisa graduated from college. I helped my sister put her wedding together, cried with her when she lost two babies, and rejoiced when she gave birth to two healthy infants.

I'm grateful my mom and dad were willing to open our home and their hearts to another daughter because it gave me the chance to open my heart to another sister — a sister of the heart!

Whoever welcomes one of these little children in my name welcomes me; and whoever welcomes me does not welcome me but the one who sent me.

MARK 9:37

63

this is what sisters do

Jill Lynnele Gregory

░░

Your sister is your mirror, shining back at you with a world of possibilities. She is your witness, who sees you at your worst and best, and loves you anyway. She is your partner in crime, your midnight companion, someone who knows when you are smiling, even in the dark. She is your teacher, your defense attorney, your personal press agent, even your shrink. Some days, she's the reason you wish you were an only child.

BARBARA ALPERT

*I*n our growing-up years my sisters and I loved to pretend to be the characters we watched on television. As the youngest, I didn't have much of a choice regarding which person I got to be. Some scenarios were okay, like *The Brady Bunch*: Leanne pretended to be Marcia, Laura took on the role of Jan, and I was Cindy. Or when we watched *Charlie's Angels*, Leanne got the part of Kelly, Laura became Sabrina, and I was, of course — Jill. Other programs weren't as much fun. When *Gilligan's Island* came on, Leanne got to be the glamorous Ginger, Laura was pretty Maryanne, and my sisters made me be Mrs. Howell. Then there was *Scooby Doo*: Leanne became Daphne, Laura acted out the role of Velma, and I, sad to say, had to be Scooby Doo — or the guest star, Phyllis Diller — or even one of the Harlem Globetrotters!

Despite my role in real life as the "little sister," I maintained a very close relationship with Leanne and Laura. As we have grown into adults, those ties have become deep, strong bonds in my life.

. . . .

When my daughter was diagnosed with autism, my life was turned upside down. One of the strongest anchors during this storm has been the love and support of my sisters. Leanne took on the role of "second mother" in my absence. She cared for my children when I took Sarah to specialists and attended conferences to help me understand my child's challenges. My sister never complained about the extra responsibility, but saw it as her way to help. She has been my buffer.

When my son was having trouble paying attention in school, my sister knew my heart could not take on one more burden. She coached him and helped him focus on his schoolwork so he could get back on track. Leanne also recruited help for me when I needed to attend a daily program for three months with my autistic daughter. She prays with me on the phone or stops by with a soda or with my favorite flavored cappuccino to encourage me to hang in there.

My other sister, Laura, is a successful manager for a large company. Her job is intense, and she often deals with heavy deadlines and important meetings. As Sarah's therapy required more time than I could give with all the other responsibilities at home, Laura did the most sacrificial thing a sister could do. She stepped down from her position to work part time, so she could assist me with the therapy Sarah requires.

Each day when Sarah comes home from her preschool for autistic children, Laura comes over to spend the rest of the day working with my daughter. This is not a glamorous job. Sarah uses very few words and often screams or throws objects to demonstrate her disapproval. As unpleasant as it is to admit, she sometimes smears her bowel movements in protest. Sarah has high energy and loves to escape and run away from us. Working with my daughter can be tiring and laborious. But she and Laura have developed a very special bond, and Sarah looks forward to her arrival.

Sarah's progress has been remarkable! She is speaking words and responding appropriately to questions. I used to cry every time Sarah did something new. Now I am in awe of how God has touched her life with steady progress in a positive direction. My sister will not accept payment for her hours of labor despite my protests. She simply says, "Jill, this is what sisters do."

. . . .

How thankful I am for two sisters who continue to play important roles in this unexpected drama in my life. The same sisters I giggled with in our bedroom during our growing-up years are the same sisters who wipe my tears now. I didn't have a choice in selecting my sisters, much like I didn't have the privilege of choosing my television characters when we were playacting as kids, but God knew how much I would need supportive sisters.

I've discovered that sisterhood is a place where needs are known, shared responsibility is embraced, tears are wiped, and joys are celebrated. It's what sisters do.

. . . .

And my God will meet all your needs according to his glorious riches in Christ Jesus.

PHILIPPIANS 4:19

kitchen patrol

Kelly King

· ·

I'll talk all day if you'll only set me going.
Beth says I never know when to stop.

LOUISA MAY ALCOTT, *LITTLE WOMEN*

The year I entered seventh grade, my mother accepted her first full-time teaching position. Accustomed to having a mother at home all day, my younger sister and I suddenly found ourselves having to help around the house more often. Although Mom still carried the majority of the cleaning responsibilities, Karen and I had the task of cleaning the kitchen each evening after dinner.

Our family had a home-cooked meal together almost every night. We would gather at the dining room table at about 5:30 p.m., and our southern culture usually dictated the menu. Often the table was piled high with chicken-fried steak, fried chicken, fried okra, or fried potatoes. As tasty as those items were, our favorite part of the meal was dessert. My mother usually baked homemade pie in the morning before she left to teach at the nearby elementary school. Dinner was never complete without dessert, but this also meant extra dirty dishes.

Karen and I soon developed a system for accomplishing our chores quickly so we could pursue other important activities — like watching *Little House on the Prairie* on television. While I cleared the table, Karen became the expert at loading the dishwasher. She could find more room in the dishwasher for an extra glass or skillet than anyone in the family.

Very soon our evening ritual became much more than "kitchen patrol." Our interests were extremely different, and we learned a lot about each other's lives over rinsing glasses and scrubbing gravy out of the saucepan. Karen's popular life was filled with cheerleading, running, and being student council president. I thought my life of piano practice, swimming, and yearbook deadlines paled in comparison to her exhilarating activities. We shared our struggles over friendships, and I secretly envied the attention she received from boys.

During my senior year of high school, the daily kitchen duties took an unexpected turn. Horror of horrors, our dishwasher broke down, and our parents informed us that instead of fixing this appliance or buying a new one, we could just wash the dishes by hand.

We took turns whining, "This is torture!"

I occasionally exploded with self-pity: "This is the seventies! No one washes dishes by hand in suburban middle America!" But we continued washing those dishes by hand. At my side, Karen would wash while I rinsed, dried, and put the dishes back in the cabinets.

Time passed, and we started facing the fact that I would be graduating and heading off to college soon. Our conversations over the kitchen sink deepened as we discussed our futures and what God had planned for our lives. One evening the conversation centered on some special meetings we had attended at church. Karen looked up and asked, "Do you ever question your faith? Do you ever wonder if you really accepted Christ as your Savior?"

I quickly prayed, "Please, God, give me the right words."

For the next fifteen minutes we discussed how we had both come to know the Lord at a very young age. I recalled sitting next to Karen in church when she leaned toward me and said, "How do I ask Jesus into my heart?"

Being at that time the older, wiser sister at ten years of age, I helped Karen pray a simple prayer of faith, asking Jesus to be the Lord of her life.

Over dirty dishes I reminded Karen that her prayer had been heard and her commitment to Christ was real. We dismissed the doubts and shared how Christ had been the One who had genuinely cleansed us from our sin. That night washing dishes seemed effortless as our attention was centered on an intimate conversation between two sisters rather than on completing a mandatory chore.

The following year I returned home from college for a weekend visit. Ready to resume the appointed task, I asked Karen if she had to do the dishes alone while I was away at school. My sister looked at me with a sparkle in her eye. "I don't have to do the dishes anymore. Mom had someone look at the dishwasher and he found out nothing was wrong with it the entire time we did those dishes by hand last year."

We laughed as we recalled the many hours of "slave labor" we had devoted to our kitchen patrol duties. However, deep in our hearts, we knew God planned our time at the kitchen sink for a far greater purpose. Two sisters grew to love each other deeply as they shared their joys, questions, and spiritual concerns at a heart level. Our "kitchen patrol" was a divine appointment in disguise.

* * *

But encourage one another daily, as long as it is called Today.

HEBREWS 3:13

a trip to france

Nancy Hanna

··

*When sisters stand shoulder to shoulder,
who stands a chance against us?*

PAM BROWN

*O*ur *much older* sister Ginna was turning fifty, so we
decided it was time for an exotic European adventure. My two sisters, two sisters-in-law, and I burned
up phone lines in five different cities planning our fantasy trip
and a much-needed break from our daily domestic bliss.

When we landed at Charles de Gaulle International Airport, a grin ignited the expression on my face, and it didn't burn
out for days. The first time I handled the money imprinted with
the faces of impressionist painters, I knew I had found *my
people*. I was giddy with childlike delight and glad I had waited
to saunter down the Champs-Elysées and hike up the Eiffel
tower until I was still younger than fifty. Finally I understood
the power of the word *wait*. If everything comes too fast or too
soon, we don't know the thrill that comes after wanting some-

thing for a long time. I sensed God's smile on me as he granted this long-desired heart wish.

For three glorious days we toured Paris. The Eiffel Tower did not disappoint us. One evening we toured the city by way of the Seine River — which turned out to be an energy-conserving way to get our directional bearings. We shopped for silk scarves, tasted crème pastries, and enjoyed an evening of dining at Le Souffle Restaurant, where lap puppies sat at the feet of their mistresses. We took a day trip to Monet's village of Giverny, and we hiked up to Sacré Coeur to see the lights of Paris twinkle.

The next day, thanks to Martha, our youngest sister, we were off on the fast train from Paris to Marseilles, headed for Aix-en-Provence. We stayed at the real deal Le Pigonnet Hotel in a bungalow we had all to ourselves. We found ourselves in a postcard-perfect medieval town.

In a flash it was time to return to Paris for one last night on the town. With bags now crammed with French treasures, stomachs cushioned in cream, and wallets emptied of the impressionists — their money, that is — we made our way back to Marseilles to catch the train. Somewhere between the gate and the train, Martha began an earnest search for her return ticket. While the five of us loaded our bags and ourselves onto the train and took our seats, Martha broke out in a cold sweat as she riffled through her books and pockets in search of the missing ticket. When the train pulled out, it became clear that there was no ticket.

We were more than halfway to Paris by the time the young man in uniform came through the car to collect our tickets. By now our party had grown tense. He took Lydia's and Kristin's tickets. Ginna gave him hers. There was a lot of *bon jour*-ing and *merci*-ing going on. Martha and I were next. At that moment the "spirit of sisterly compassion and creativity" came upon me. I told Martha not to say a word, but to just look sad and nod at whatever I said — to nod *a lot*. She looked at me as if I were some kind of crazy woman (which she already knew was true). Then it was *show time*!

Having worked in the theater, I knew how to be dramatic. I assumed my "forlorn woman-in-distress" pose and spoke to the man with intensified feminine charm and deep urgency. "We have a problem and I'm sure you can help us solve it . . ." I knew, as any actor does, it was my moment on life's stage to play my part most sincerely and with great vigor.

"A problem?" said the man in uniform.

I handed him the purchase receipt we found, showing our purchase of five train tickets.

"Ah, yes, as you see by our receipt, we purchased *five*." I pointed to the five of us. "We are traveling together and all of us have our tickets — except for my little sister. She lost hers. I *know* you can help us. In fact, we're leaving France tomorrow, and we're just heartbroken about it."

Without smiling, he said, "Departing the country tomorrow?"

"*Oui*. We spent all our money, bought many beautiful things, but now we must go." I let the words linger in the air as I saw him weighing his options.

"Well, I suppose if you're leaving tomorrow . . ."

"*Oui. Oui,*" I assured him. "And we will have great memories to take home with us."

I tried not to speak my afterthought aloud: . . . *especially if you let us off the hook for the cost of the ticket.* I wanted to beg, but the new French scarf knotted around my neck gave me the determination to stick to my air of nonchalant confidence in the Parisian style we had observed during our trip.

"If you leave tomorrow then," he said, handing back my ticket with a bit of a scolding look.

"*Merci,* we'll be out of here," I assured him.

And off he went!

Martha shook her head in disbelief at the results of my melodramatic performance.

We looked up at three pairs of large sister eyes staring at us. "Well?" asked the sisters.

"Done!" I declared.

"*Magnifique!*" they exclaimed.

The American damsels had conquered the French. As long as we were leaving the country the next day, he forgave us for our lost ticket. Though bone-tired from all the fun, I had to grin. God is not only in the center of our small stuff and our quiet needs, he's in the middle of our indulgences as well. *Bon jour!*

. . . .

Therefore we do not lose heart. Though outwardly we are wasting away, yet inwardly we are being renewed day by day.

2 CORINTHIANS 4:16

timely advice

Bonnie Afman Emmorey

....

*There can be no situation in life in which the conversation of my
dear sister will not administer some comfort to me.*

LADY MARY WORTLEY MONTAGU

*I*t was too soon. I wasn't ready. My son Nathan was only fourteen. How could this have happened?

Nate was a freshman in high school, and the homecoming dance was just around the corner, but I wasn't worried. Nate was way too shy to ask a girl out on a date. We were *years* away from *that* problem.

What I wasn't prepared for was the aggressive girl who asked *him* to take her to this grand event. Without even checking with me, Nate accepted her invitation. I was in a dither! He was too young and innocent.

It was time to call an expert — my sister Carol. She had already been through this first date and "aggressive girl stuff" with *her* son, and she lived to tell about it. I knew she would have the wisdom to walk me through this new challenge. I made the call, hoping she would tell me Nate was too young and this date should be canceled. Wrong! She told me Nate's peer relationships in his class might be jeopardized if I stepped in and forced him to break the date. This was a very popular girl who had already turned down two other young men before contacting Nathan.

Carol reminded me that Nate and his date were only fourteen, and they would need a driver. Aahhh! That sister of mine is one smart cookie! She suggested that I become that driver. Yes, it would mean shuttling a couple of overdressed, under-aged nervous teenagers to and fro, but I would know what was happening at every moment.

Things were going along smoothly when the second shoe fell. They had plans for *after* the dance. They wanted to go to a friend's house to watch a video and have an after-dance party. Whoa! Now I was back to my initial feelings of fear. He was *way* too young! Once again a quick call to my sister was in order.

Carol said, "Bonnie, just ask Nate to call the girl and find out what video they will be watching." Once again, I saw the wisdom in her words. Nate was mortified with my request, but I was unyielding. He knew I was the one who could stop the whole thing, so he broke down and made the call. I overheard him ask the question, making sure that his date understood that it was his *mom* who requested the information. Fortunately, the video was one I had seen and approved, so it wasn't a problem, and the plans for the date progressed.

Fifteen minutes later the phone rang. It was the mother of Nate's date. She introduced herself to me and said, "When I heard that Nathan's mother had to know the name of the movie, I knew I was going to like this boy. He must come from a good family." She had been having the same anxieties I was experiencing. We had a lovely chat, and both of us felt better about the evening.

The girl I thought might be overly aggressive turned out to be a lovely, reserved young woman. She just knew the type of young man she wanted to date and decided it was worth the risk to make it happen.

The young people enjoyed their evening together. Nate survived his first date, and so did both sets of parents and one concerned Aunt Carol. I'm not sure how many times I called my sister that night as I kept her up-to-date on how the evening was going. But she was there for me. Even though we don't live in the same city, it's good to have a sister who is only a phone call away.

My son Nathan is now well into his twenties, and I know he feels free to call his Aunt Carol and tell her all about his latest date. I'm no longer the only one to have her on speed dial. We've both learned that God speaks through the wisdom of godly people.

* *

Let the wise listen and add to their learning,
and let the discerning get guidance.

PROVERBS 1:5

a sister with a secret

Charlotte Adelsperger

What did you do today that only a Christian would have done?

CORRIE TEN BOOM

*a*s teenagers my twin sister Alberta and I shared many common interests — tennis, softball, and a lot of the same friends. However, one warm summer afternoon Alberta took off on a bike ride by herself. Hours went by, and I began to wonder where she was. At suppertime when she finally returned, her face looked hot and her eyes pensive.

"Hey, you were gone a *long time*," I remarked.

"Yeah, it turned out to be a long ride," she said. Then she switched to another subject.

I let it go, knowing she'd tell me about it sometime. Alberta shared just about everything. But this time — nothing.

Days later Alberta and I sat cross-legged on our beds talking about kids at church and what we wanted to do the next day. Alberta dropped her voice to a whisper.

"Remember the day I went on the bike ride?" she began.

"Sure do," I said, studying her eyes.

"Well, I went someplace. Something kept coming to my mind, but I wasn't sure how it would work out."

"Tell me!" I blurted out.

"You know Margaret, the girl our pastor told about in church? He said she'd love to have visitors. So I took along Margaret's address. I kept riding — and praying — until I came to her street. Then I took a deep breath and rang the doorbell."

"Oh," I said in amazement. "What was it like?"

"Well, her parents were very nice, and they were thrilled I came. They took me to Margaret's room. She was in bed. You'd like her — she's so sweet and cheerful. We talked and talked. She wants to meet *you* too!"

"I want to meet *her*," I said. "Alberta, I think God must have sent you that day."

My sister's face brightened as she told me more about Margaret's personality. I sensed Alberta's loving enthusiasm. We decided to go together to see Margaret as soon as possible.

The very next day we pedaled our bikes to Margaret's front door. As her parents greeted us, any apprehension I may have had seemed to vanish. I was with my encouraging, caring sister — and she led the way to Margaret's room.

Margaret was gaunt and frail, propped up in a hospital bed in her little room. And for the first time, I saw what the horrid disease of polio had done to this young person. Margaret's body was completely paralyzed. But her eyes danced as she spoke, using short, shallow breaths. Her face radiated joy as she spent time with girls her own age.

Alberta's compassion taught me to focus on the personhood of someone who is ill or handicapped. It didn't take long to discover Margaret's hobby. She loved movie stars, and she had compiled a number of scrapbooks filled with pictures of her favorite actors and actresses. During later visits we brought her movie magazines. Sometimes we cut out pictures she wanted of stars like Gene Kelly, Judy Garland, and John Wayne.

The three of us also talked about our faith and about how God is always with us. Alberta and I promised to keep praying for Margaret. Her face was radiant as she told how our pastor had come to see her almost every week since she was diagnosed with polio. He was so full of Christ's love and his visits lifted her spirits.

A year later Alberta and I got our drivers' licenses, and we celebrated by inviting Margaret to go with us to a drive-in theater. Due to her illness, she was not allowed in crowded places (like an indoor theater), and she really looked forward to this outing.

"She can go when she's over her cold," her mother told us. The plan was that her father would lift Margaret into our car, and the three of us would embark on our adventure.

But early one morning our pastor phoned. I took the call. Margaret had been fighting respiratory infections, and her lungs were weak.

"Our dear Margaret has lost her earthly battle," he said reverently, "but she's with the Lord in heaven now."

My throat tightened, and I shook all over as the pastor continued. "It would mean so much to the family if you and your sister could be at her service," he said. "I think you were the only young people from church who visited her. She spoke so fondly of you both."

Teary-eyed, Alberta and I attended the memorial service for our valiant friend. It was our first funeral, and it was very emotional. But we experienced it together, stronger now and in deeper fellowship with God because one of us had taken a risk on a summer day. A long bike ride.

But when you give to the needy, do not let your left hand know what your right hand is doing, so that your giving may be in secret. Then your Father, who sees what is done in secret, will reward you.

MATTHEW 6:3 – 4

joined at the hip

Cynthia Reynolds

* *

Close to my heart you'll always be.
Friends forever, my sister and me.

FOUND ON A PLAQUE IN A GIFT SHOP

*M*y little brother Darin chuckled as my sister and I walked by with our arms around each other. "You two are always together," he said. "It's like you're joined at the hip!"

My sister Patti and I looked at each other as if we had just received a knock on the door from the Publisher's Clearinghouse spokesman. "Joined at the hip!" we chortled. We bumped hips and swayed through the house in rhythm, trying to walk as close together as possible. No one paid much attention. The fun was all ours.

But we weren't always "joined at the hip." I was seven years old when my sister Patti was born. We called her our little "Patticake." As she lay there small and helpless, I wondered if she would ever be big enough to play hopscotch with me or run around on summer evenings catching fireflies as the light of day faded into night in our little town in Iowa. Would she and I ever be friends? I felt very protective of her tiny little hands and feet, her curly golden brown hair, and her twinkling eyes.

She was not quite two when we moved halfway across the country to California. *That's okay*, I thought. *I'll be able to look after her.* And look after her I did! My mom and dad both needed to work, and I was just old enough to be the babysitter for my little sister. This arrangement was okay for a while — until I turned twelve — and then my little sister began to cramp my style.

All my friends were taking off for the beach that summer, and I was stuck in a house with no air-conditioning and a five-year-old little sister to watch. I wanted to put on my new two-piece bathing suit my mom had a fit about me buying. I longed to stretch out on my stunning beach towel and check out the boys through my new pink sunglasses. But instead of having fun, I was watching *Captain Kangaroo* and fending off the ice-cream man. And it was all Patti's fault! I resented having to stay home when I knew I was missing out on all the fun I could have had with my friends.

Then, just about the time Patti was old enough to be on her own, my younger brother was born and I took care of him too. When I turned nineteen, I was too restless to stay around any-more. It was Patti's turn to be the babysitter! A few years later I married, moved away, and left her. Our parents were struggling and, before long, they divorced. Patti was only fourteen. But I had my own life with my wonderful husband. He was studying for the ministry, and we were starting a family and doing overseas missions work. It seemed I had much more important things to do than wait for my sister to grow up.

Three years passed and I was living in Munich, Germany. The phone rang. It was my mother's voice on the other end of the line. "Patti's had an accident!" My heart stopped momentarily as my mind raced wildly through all kinds of possibilities. "She was cutting the grass and tried to pull a stick out of the lawnmower, when her fingers got caught in the blades. The doctor thinks he can reattach her fingers, but there will be nerve damage."

My heart was racing at supersonic speed. After hearing more details about the accident and conveying my love and concern to my sister via my mom, I hung up the phone and slumped on the couch. The memory of my sister's baby fingers curling around my thumb sent a wave of pain through my body. *I should be there for her*, I thought. *But would she want me?* The gap between us suddenly seemed to be about *more* than time and space, and it made my heart ache.

I broke down in prayer. "Lord, I am here doing the work you called me to do, but I've missed out on knowing my own sister." My thoughts were rambling:

What's she like?

Does she love me?

Does she ever think about me?

Is it too late for me to "be there" for her and to be her friend?

On our next trip to the United States we went to visit family, and I was nervous. For some reason all I could think about was how mean I had been to Patti so many years ago. I had moved away and never looked back. I walked into her home and there on the wall was a "sister plaque" I had sent her several years before. On the lamp table I saw a framed picture of the two of us, and I knew in a heartbeat that we were joined by stronger ties than time and space could ever destroy.

"There you are!" she said exuberantly as she came rushing across the room with her arms outstretched. I looked into her face and knew she was my "Patti-cake." Although time and distance had separated us, we were still joined at the heart.

"Hey, you two," Darin joked, "you *do* separate when you go to the bathroom, don't you?"

It was good to laugh along with everyone else. We were apart for a few minutes — but then we were right back together with our arms around each other, just as we were in days gone by.

I still live far away from my little sister, and her life is burdened with painful troubles I can hardly imagine. But now we pick up the phone more often, and when I hear her voice I know we are connected — "joined at the heart" until we can be "joined at the hip" once again.

* * *

May the Lord keep watch between you and me
when we are away from each other.

Genesis 31:49

87

lavish lips

Carol Kent

. . . .

*A smile is a light in the window of your face that shows
that your heart is at home.*

AUTHOR UNKNOWN

*M*y sister Paula and I have something special in common, but I never learned the value of our "sameness" until we were almost grown.

It all started in fourth grade. I was sitting in my seat, staring at the front of the classroom, priding myself on being a good student, when I felt a tap on my shoulder.

The young man in the seat behind me was named John, and I'd had a crush on him since the first day of school. He had eyes to die for and all the girls were longing for a lingering glance from him. I put on my best smile and lowered my eyes and my voice as I turned and softly said, "Yes?"

I waited. He said nothing. He simply stared at something on my face. His elbow tapped the fellow seated next to him and he said, "Do you see what I mean?"

This student also started staring at something on my face and I heard him respond, "Oh, yeah, I see it."

John, still staring at my face but not directly into my eyes, said, "She *does* have big lips, doesn't she?"

At that moment my ego deflated, my heart raced, and I felt a nervous, blotchy rash creep up my neck and publicly announce my personal humiliation to the classmates who were in full view of this unpleasant scene.

I turned around in my seat and pretended it didn't matter, but I was devastated. I lived through to the end of that painful day and found a quiet seat in the back of the bus.

When the bus pulled up in front of my house, I ran through the front door, charged up the stairs to my bedroom, and wailed like a woman with a broken heart. I was convinced I would never be asked out on a date. I knew I would never get married because in our culture, if you don't get dates you don't get proposals. I was sure I would never be hired for gainful employment because of my grotesquely large lips.

My campaign to become one of the thin-lipped people began. I spent hours in front of my vanity mirror, taking on the difficult task of rolling my lips in so they would look thinner. The next step was to learn how to speak with skinny lips. This was no small challenge. My words were distorted, and my sisters taunted me with, "What are you doing to your mouth? You look funny and we can't understand you."

I spent several years trying to make my lips smaller and "more beautiful" because of a hurtful comment from a boy in my fourth grade class. Thankfully, I eventually grew up and my face finally grew into my oversized mouth.

Years later my sister Paula and I laughed out loud as we realized both of us had been "blessed" with large lips. We discovered women were paying big bucks to get collagen injections in their lips, and movie stars like Julia Roberts made big lips fashionable. With a twinkle in her eye and an audible chuckle, my outrageously fun sister suggested, "Maybe we should get our lips tattooed, so when we are little old ladies, we won't have to worry about getting our lip liner on straight."

Actually, that's not a bad idea. However, we have both decided that having a smile on our lips is much more important than the size of our lips!*

. . . .

*A cheerful heart brings a smile to your face;
a sad heart makes it hard to get through the day.*

PROVERBS 15:13 MSG

---

* Adapted from *Speak Up With Confidence*, by Carol Kent, copyright © 1997. Used by permission of NavPress, www.navpress.com. All rights reserved.

a closet full of joy

Bonnie Afman Emmorey

. . . .

A good laugh is sunshine in a house.

WILLIAM MAKEPEACE THACKERAY

When our mother was forty-two, she announced to the family that she was pregnant. All of us were surprised. Mother and Dad already had five children, ranging in age from Carol, who was seventeen years old, down to our only brother, Ben, who had recently turned four. I didn't tell anyone, but I secretly prayed for another boy. That way I would retain my standing as "the baby girl" of the family. It wasn't much, but at least it was better than just being "Daughter #4."

When July came that year, mother delivered "Daughter #5," and they named her Joy. I wasn't happy. At the tender age of nine, I was jealous of all the attention this darling blonde baby sister was getting from everyone. However, over the next several years, my attitude changed dramatically as little "Joy Joy" captured my heart. We often said her first name twice because it described her joy-filled personality so well. Joy and I could always make each other laugh.

When she began her university studies, I was already an *old* married woman. It was no surprise that beautiful Joy had a string of beaus, but soon tall, handsome Kelly stood out from the rest. Before long, our baby sister fell in love and accepted a proposal from the man of her dreams.

To my surprise, Joy asked *me* to be her matron of honor. My little sister was so busy with her classes that she asked me to plan her wedding. I enthusiastically accepted the assignment. Mother and Dad were in full-time ministry, and they had *five* daughters. Finances were tight. But I was up for the challenge of creating a beautiful wedding on a shoestring budget.

We knew our mother had our grandmother's antique white wedding dress and that her sister (Aunt Kay) had the original bridesmaid's dress. After digging through the closet, we found the wedding dress, and Aunt Kay quickly sent the matching attendant's gown. We decided that with a little effort, we could make these dresses work for Joy's wedding. However, we had a challenge — Grandma and her bridesmaid had worn corsets and they each had seventeen-inch waistlines. We soon discovered that with new cummerbunds, those dresses would look like they were made for *us*. Joy's beautiful wedding day was filled with old and new memories.

As grown-up sisters we continued an earlier passion — shopping — and we've been known to hit resale shops and bargain basements with great gusto. Since Joy's husband is a pastor and she now has seven children, finances are sometimes challenging. One day I was in my closet contemplating the various "sizes of my life" when I got an idea. Joy should come to *my* closet on a shopping trip. I had way too many clothes.

I called Joy and invited her to come on an "all-expenses-paid shopping trip" — to my closet. Since I live three hours away and she has a house full of children, we had to plan this shopping trip carefully. Joy and her daughter (my niece, Carol Joy) arrived at eleven at night and we sat around the kitchen table planning our shopping strategy for the next day. We talked, laughed, and reminisced over our many past shopping experiences.

It was time to set the guidelines for this unusual shopping trip. It was my closet we would be diving into, and I knew there could be problems. Joy is a very stylish, up-to-date, fashionable woman, and she *has* to be. She has a teenage daughter. My closets are filled with clothes that are more than twenty-five years old. I tend to buy clothes that are a bit unusual and no one knows *when* or *if* they ever *were* in style. I have always enjoyed being a "trendsetter" rather than a "fashion follower," and I knew there could be the danger of ridicule from my younger sister and from her very fashionable daughter. So I made the rules. Each of them would be allowed up to, but not to exceed, three laughs. If they passed their limit, the shopping trip to my closet would end. They looked dubious, but I was unyielding. My fragile pride was at stake. We finally went to bed and drifted off to sleep.

Morning dawned and the fun began. The closet doors swung open and the fashion show started. That day we laughed until tears ran down our cheeks. I soon gave up on counting the laughs. (I know my little sister tried to be gracious when she found my purple harem pants and the abbreviated matching jacket.) We were making memories, and we both knew it.

Time passes, but one thing remains the same. "Joy Joy" is still living up to the meaning of her name, and she continues to remind me that laughter is the best medicine. Her example helps me to value the memories of the past, to savor our good times together, and to treasure our Christian heritage. And it's no secret — whether in a mall or in the back of a closet, Joy brings much sunshine to our shopping experiences.

* * *

I have indeed received much joy and encouragement from your love, because the hearts of the saints have been refreshed through you.

PHILEMON 7 NRSV

one of my toughest choices

Traci Ausborn

For there is no friend like a sister
In calm or stormy weather;
To cheer one on the tedious way,
To fetch one if one goes astray,
To lift one if one totters down,
To strengthen whilst one stands.

CHRISTINA ROSSETTI

ow stupid are you?" my sister asked.

Through sobs I replied, "I guess pretty stupid."

Actually it seemed like the thing to do at the time. I was a young married woman with a son almost a year old and I had a great job. My boss had decided to fly me to one of his offices in North Carolina to see the facility and to train some staff members. I was excited. It was an opportunity not many professional women my age were given.

After weeks of preparation and carefully executed lists, my husband knew when to pick up the baby, what types of diapers to buy, what phone numbers he could use to reach me, when to feed the dogs, and what days he needed to put the trash out. I was ready for this trip.

A teary good-bye at the airport gate left me exhausted and wondering why I would put myself through this exasperating anguish for three days of work clear across the country. I walked onto the airplane, said a weak "Hello" to the flight attendant, and found my seat. I was lost in my thoughts when the flight attendant's voice caught my attention.

"Miss, are you okay?"

At the time I didn't realize I was experiencing a panic attack. I felt like I couldn't breathe. Terror seized me. We hadn't even left the ground yet!

"No!" I gasped. She motioned to a coworker, requesting assistance. With both of them invading what little air I had around me, I managed to choke out the words: "I need to get off the plane."

I have no idea how they did it. I don't remember walking down the concourse, but I found myself back where I'd started — at the same spot where I had left my husband and my son. However, things had changed. My family was gone and I was no longer breathing freely.

"Should we call 9-1-1?" one of the flight attendants asked. "She's turning blue."

I'm certain I was by that point, but I could feel my head beginning to clear.

"No, I'll be fine," I said, as reassuringly as possible. "Can you get my luggage off the plane?"

"You're not getting back on the plane?"

Stunned at the thought, I managed a calm, "I don't think so."

Through a series of events that are still hazy to me, I eventually made it home. Not having the courage to face my boss yet, I needed to talk to my sister. I longed for her listening ear, support, and love.

"You got off the plane?" she asked. "I can't believe you got off the plane. This was a great opportunity for you and *you got off the plane?*"

Ouch, that hurt. So much for sisterly support!

We talked for several minutes and eventually the shock wore off. I realized my sister loved me enough to ask me a question that meant more to me than just the obvious. "Why didn't you want to go?" she queried.

I never considered not going, but deep inside me I couldn't do it. Her targeted questions launched a soul-searching within me:

What is it I want to be?

What drives me?

What really matters?

Am I willing to be away from my baby for multiple-day trips to further my career?

Do I need this experience to feel important?

My sister wasn't judging or condemning me; she was just challenging me to look at the motives behind my actions. She loved me in that moment by asking the hard questions and helped me to evaluate what really mattered in my life.

I remained at the same company, in that same position, for ten years. During that time, my boss supported me completely in what was then, and remains today, my first priority — motherhood. He chuckled over the airplane story.

The choice to keep my family a priority has kept me close to home. I occasionally speak at conferences and retreats, but I work those events around the sports and school events of my children. This choice has been right for me. My sister knew me well enough to recognize what I hadn't realized yet — on the day I made one of my toughest choices on an airplane.

. . . .

Speaking the truth in love, we will in all things grow up into him who is the Head, that is, Christ. From him the whole body, joined and held together by every supporting ligament, grows and builds itself up in love, as each part does its work.

EPHESIANS 4:15 – 16

98

three sisters and
a butcher knife

Page Hughes

· ·

Is solace anywhere more comforting than in the arms of a sister?

ALICE WALKER

ut Mom, we're afraid of the dark."

At two, three, and four years of age, my sisters and I had vivid imaginations that played tricks on us when we went to bed. The bushes outside our bedroom windows cast shadows that danced on our walls when the moon was bright. The shadows looked like boogeymen to us, and we often ran to our parents' bedroom, begging them to let us climb into their bed.

"Girls, get back in your beds. You know the Lord is with you, and he is going to take care of you. Remember our verse: 'When I am afraid, I will trust in you. In God, whose word I praise.'*

---

* Psalm 56:3–4.

During those dark, fearful nights, Gina, Dawn, and I would toddle back to bed whispering, "When I am afraid, I will trust in you. In God, whose word I praise."

This verse continued to be a comfort to us even as we grew older. One evening when we were young teenagers, Mom and Dad went out for a short time and left us at home. Gina was in charge. As the oldest sister, she was responsible for taking care of the rest of us. The house was locked and we were safe. Then Gina thought she heard a strange sound outside. She ran to get Dawn and me and asked in a hushed whisper, "Did you girls hear anything?"

Wide-eyed with fear, we said, "N–n–n–no."

Gina whispered, "I think someone is out there. Follow me and we'll get away from all of the windows." We quickly and quietly made our way to a corner in the kitchen, a place that wasn't visible from any window. Gina opened a drawer and pulled out a large, sharp butcher knife. Then our big sister instructed us to take turns saying the Bible verse: "When I am afraid, I will trust in you. In God, whose word I praise."

We carefully followed Gina's instructions and walked around in our tight circle at least four times, taking turns quoting our "comfort verse." We then sat down and prayed together, asking God to protect us from whatever adversary waited outside our door.

Within a few minutes Mom and Dad arrived and wondered what in the world we were doing sitting in a circle clutching a butcher knife. We all took a deep breath, relieved and thankful for the security and presence of our parents.

Mom and Dad chuckled a little, but reassured us there was no reason for fear. They were concerned about our use of a knife for protection, but they also encouraged us that we had done the right thing by calling upon God and resting on his word to calm our fears.

Since that evening my sisters and I have had plenty of additional fearful experiences: we've lost children, endured financial stress, and dealt with challenging family relationship issues. Each time one of these fearful situations invades our lives, we go back to the verse we learned as babes, practiced as children, and live by today: "When I am afraid, I will trust in you. In God, whose word I praise." When we repeat those words, God gives us peace in the middle of life's storms.

. . . .

The Lord is my light and my salvation — whom shall I fear? The Lord is the stronghold of my life — of whom shall I be afraid?

PSALM 27:1

angel face

Carol Kent

Courage is not the towering oak that sees storms come and go;
it is the fragile blossom that opens in the snow.

ALICE MACKENZIE SWAIM

*M*y husband and I had been married for two years when his father and stepmother announced that they were going to have a baby. No one had expected another sibling to enter this already very large family. However, it didn't take long before all of us were anticipating the birth of this little sister.

Lori came into this world on a day filled with sunshine, and her presence in a room always made the atmosphere brighter. I was sure I saw her smile when she was still an infant, but when you have a vivid imagination (and I do), I admit her "smile" may actually have been a facial contortion caused by a feeling of gas.

As Lori grew, she seemed to have trouble breathing; she coughed and had lung infections frequently. Tests revealed that my five-year-old sister-in-law had an inherited disease called "cystic fibrosis" that affects the respiratory and digestive systems along with the pancreas and the sebaceous glands. Soon the negative aspects of the disease were wreaking havoc in her tiny body. Her lungs produced thick, sticky mucus that not only kept her from breathing normally, it often blocked the bowel and produced great discomfort.

After the diagnosis, Lori began a wide variety of treatments. Sometimes there were debates about whether the *cure* was more cruel than the disease. At an early age this lung-wasting disease had to be treated with drugs that produced a barrel chest and a huge belly on her little thirty-two-pound body. Lori was always "a little lady" and she struggled with not feeling as pretty as she had once been. The steroids enlarged her face and the tips of her fingers became like large blue pads.

The disease attacked like a predator, but at the age of eight, Lori made a choice. She determined not to give in to the depression and the discouragement of a terminal illness. Her chipper voice could be heard as she joked with her physicians, "You know, doctor, I'm going to charge *you* for this visit. If you go through with this examination, you'll owe me fifty cents!" The doctors loved Lori and often lingered long after the examinations were completed. Being in her presence was a gift of life and love.

Lori often would lie on a board, elevated at one end in order to drain her lungs and improve her breathing. Whenever

I tried to comfort her, I'd hear Lori's sweet voice say, "Don't worry about it. I'll be okay." She joked with her siblings and joined in the fun of each moment.

As month followed month, her physical condition grew progressively worse. I walked in one afternoon and my then ten-year-old sister-in-law looked up and smiled. "Hi, Carol. I'm so glad you came. I've been talking to God a lot lately and I'll be going to see him soon."

"What makes you think *that*?" I quipped back, with fresh tears clouding my vision.

"I just know," she said with a smile. "It's almost time."

That day there was an angelic glow around this precious child. Her facial expression exuded a quiet confidence that God was in control of her destiny, and even if her life was short, it had been a great ride. I felt comforted and calm as her peaceful spirit positively impacted my own response to her critical condition.

Lori was with her parents on the day God called her home. A smile outlined her lips and Lori's arms were raised in an upward direction. It was as if angels had come to carry her safely into the arms of Jesus.

Precious in the sight of the Lord is the death of his saints.

PSALM 116:15

christmas eve competition

Bonnie Afman Emmorey

....

There is only one pretty child in the world, and every mother has it.

CHINESE PROVERB

*I*t was Christmas Eve and we gathered at Mother and Dad's house for our reunion. My four sisters and their families had been coming in at various times all day, and now everyone who could make it had arrived.

The holidays have always been a joyful time of year, and as we added little ones to the Afman family tribe, a new tradition evolved — the Christmas Eve Talent Show, featuring our gifted offspring. All of the young cousins participated, and my sisters and I eagerly watched our children perform. The talent was varied — sometimes our progeny would sing a solo or play a recital piece on the piano. There might be a karate demonstration or a display of artwork. Sometimes a sports video was played or a winning medal was displayed.

One year my nephew Josh quoted Luke 2:1–20 from memory, without any coaching. My sister Jennie then told with pride that he had been asked to recite it in the church Christmas program. That was the same year my son Nathan sang "Skateboardin' Santa." It was spirited and cute, and by the end of the song we were all joining in and singing the refrain right along with Nate. However, it seemed glaringly obvious to me that my sisters were comparing my son's public school education with my nephew's Christian school training. I admit that on some of those Christmas Eves my sisters and I felt some competition as we compared the performances of our children.

That night after the talent show had been completed, everyone was exhausted, but still wide awake with the excitement of Christmas morning just a few hours away. The cousins were all lined up in their sleeping bags on the floor, and we had just finished kissing each face and tucking the children in with love.

One of my sisters said, "Why don't we have the kids all say their bedtime prayers together?"

I experienced a momentary twinge of panic. *How would my kids' prayers compare to the prayers of their spiritual cousins?* This situation could make me look pretty bad. My children were the only ones not enrolled in a Christian school.

One by one each child prayed. The prayers were all sounding very similar when Jordan, my youngest, had his turn. *He's only four,* I reminded myself. I tried to relax my tense stomach muscles.

Jordan began his prayer, "Jesus . . ." (Oh no! What a way to start! Not even a "*Dear* Jesus.") The knot in my stomach grew tighter.

He continued. "Jesus, tomorrow's your birthday. Thank you for everything you've done for me all these years . . ."

My sister Jennie turned to me with a smile and whispered, "I want to trade sons." In my heart I did a victory march. *Yes! Yes! Yes! I won!* I couldn't believe it. All of my sisters knew that I had won the prayer competition. I was thrilled! My child had come through in the clutch. We pulled out a solid win. I found myself gleefully thinking, *My kid prayed better than* your *kid*.

At that moment I wasn't aware of how similar my response was to the proud and arrogant Pharisee (Luke 18:10–14), and I enjoyed my sister's response to my son's prayer. I'm sure Christ rejoiced in Jordan's innocent conversational tone, but it didn't take long for me to realize my jubilation in winning the prayer competition grieved my Lord deeply. I needed to pray that night too — a prayer of confession.

The cousins are almost grown now, but when I'm tempted to compare myself with my sisters or my children with their children, my mind goes back to one Christmas Eve when I learned an important lesson in humility.

. . . .

For all those who exalt themselves will be humbled,
and those who humble themselves will be exalted.

LUKE 18:14 TNIV

oh, bring us some kitty pudding

Allison L. Shaw

. . . .

Laughter is God's medicine, the most beautiful therapy
God ever gave humanity.

AUTHOR UNKNOWN

I am a Canadian citizen who married a California boy
and moved far away from home. One of the fringe
benefits of marrying my wonderful husband was that
I was finally going to have my very own sister! I have two brothers and my sister-in-law Kelly has two brothers, so this marriage
was going to work out well for *both* of us. Kelly had been pro-
moting my addition to the family since she was ten years old, and
I was equally excited to have another girl on my family roster.

I adore my in-laws, and I have grown to love California, but
at Christmastime, I yearn for the holly-and-ivy snow-filled traditions of my childhood. What I miss the most about the holidays at home is my Grandma Marge's Christmas pudding.

Every year we would gather at my grandparents' home for Christmas dinner, and Grandma would always make the pudding. It is a rich dessert for a sophisticated palate, but even as a very young child, I adored it. Christmas just isn't Christmas without Grandma's pudding.

And that is why, during my first Shaw family Christmas in San Diego, I was suddenly homesick for Christmas pudding. I called my grandma to get the recipe and while she was glad to give it, she paused for a moment and then said, "Honey, this isn't really the kind of thing that you *start* on Christmas Eve." But I could not be daunted.

The challenge now was to find suet — on Christmas Eve — in San Diego. For those who are unfamiliar with suet, it's fat. Grandma always used the fat trimmed from around the kidneys of a cow. Since I have known my in-laws since I was sixteen years old, most of my silly schemes and Canadian capers no longer surprise them.

It was while I was on the phone explaining to the butcher at the grocery store that I needed a cup of kidney fat that my new sister-by-marriage, Kelly, walked into the kitchen. Turning to my mother-in-law with a look of horror she exclaimed, *"Kitty fat? She's making the pudding with kitty fat?"*

And thus, my favorite Christmas dish was instantly dubbed "Kitty Pudding." At a moment when I was desperate for a taste of home, my new and much-loved sister Kelly reminded me that new memories were ripe for the making. Now if I could just get the guys to muffle their *meow*ing as they partake, Christmas dinner would be absolutely purr-fect.

....

The cheerful heart has a continual feast.

PROVERBS 15:15

the poinsettia parade

Anne Denmark

....

Friends are family you choose for yourself.

JANE ADDAMS

J love Christmas. Celebrating the season has always delighted me to the core of my being. After our family moved to the United States, I initiated a new tradition to share the season with my parents, who were still living in Canada. On the first day of December I took great delight in ordering a magnificent poinsettia to be delivered to my parents' home. My mom loved decorating for Christmas, but had a limited holiday budget. I knew that this bright splash of red would be a joyful start to her holiday season.

Mom would call as soon as the poinsettia arrived and say, "Oh, Anne, it's just beautiful!" She would tell me each little detail about where she would display it and we would share our plans and dreams for the holiday season. We enjoyed this annual ritual as the kickoff to our Christmas season every year—and each year Mom said the poinsettia I had delivered was the prettiest one I had ever sent, the prettiest she had ever seen.

But the Christmas of 2001 was going to be different. The sudden deaths of my mom and dad in the spring of the year had left me broken and numb. This would be the first Christmas I had ever known without my parents. I knew my precious folks were now smiling from heaven's balcony, but their absence from my life had left a lonely chill. I wasn't looking forward to the festivities. I wasn't in the mood for celebration, and I was too weary to pretend. Grief has a way of shutting you down, and I dreaded the familiar memories and family traditions that would only intensify the ache of my loss.

The young married women in the Bible class that my husband and I taught knew that I was still working through the deep anguish of losing both of my parents within days of each other. I have no biological sisters, and throughout that spring these friends found tender ways to be like family to me and to provide a safe place for my tears. One of these precious women invited me to lunch and listened as I shared stories about my mom, including our Christmas poinsettia tradition.

Her eyes filled with tears as I told her how much I would miss sending the poinsettia and receiving the phone call from my mother. I was thankful to have the summer days ahead of me before the loneliness of the holidays set in.

But life moved on, and I soon forgot about that conversation. When the first day of December arrived, I busied myself in doing Saturday morning chores around the house. The door-bell rang and I suspected that it might be one of the neighbor-hood children selling wrapping paper or chocolates for a school fundraiser.

When I opened the door, there stood the young women from our Bible class, each one holding a bright red poinsettia in her arms. They came to honor a beloved tradition. They had not forgotten my sorrow.

That day I experienced the love of sisterhood. Into the poverty of my grieving soul flooded a love that ran deeper than girl talk and friendship. These sisters in Christ entered into my family tradition and gave it back to me as only sisters could.

As my heart surrendered to the impact of their remem-brance I began to sob, "I miss my parents so much." My sisters surrounded me with love, and they wept too. Then the poin-settia parade poured into my home and filled it with the warmth of Christ's love. It was the prettiest display I've ever seen.

Rejoice with those who rejoice, weep with those who weep.

ROMANS 12:15 NRSV

a tent and a purse
full of rocks

Pam Cronk

• •

When sisters stand shoulder to shoulder,
who stands a chance against us?

PAM BROWN

*I*t was the summer of 1969, and I had just earned my bachelor of science degree in elementary education. I was looking forward to my first year of teaching in the fall, but summers in the Upper Peninsula of Michigan are exquisitely beautiful, and I thought it was time for an adventure before embarking on my first *real* job in the classroom. My younger sister, Lois, and two cousins (both named Kathy), and I gathered our camping gear and headed for a favorite spot along the shores of crystal clear Ottawa Lake, not far from our hometown of Iron River.

We had a relaxing week of cooking meals in the great outdoors on a Coleman stove and listening to the loons' calls echoing across the lake each morning. At night the howling of the wolves awakened us at odd hours. We were having a *great* time — playing marathon games of Yahtzee and Aggravation by lamplight, singing our favorite fifties and sixties songs, scaring each other in the dark, and laughing until our sides hurt. In the evenings we sat by our cozy campfire and watched bats dive for bugs. My sister and I were enjoying this time with our cousins.

Midway through the week we went shopping in a resort town about twenty miles away so I could look for some professional clothes for my new job. When we got back to the lake, we decided to go for a refreshing swim before returning to the campsite. I parked my '56 Chevy in the parking lot, locked the doors, and the four of us went into the changing house. Following a short swim, we grabbed our beach towels and quickly changed into dry clothing.

As we approached the car, I noticed broken glass on the ground. I was amazed to see that the small vent window on the driver's door was broken! "What on earth happened?" I exclaimed. Upon further investigation, we found that my sister's purse was missing along with a piece of luggage and some clothes I had purchased on our shopping excursion that day.

We had been *robbed*!

My practical sister said, "We'd better call Mom and Dad." So we called home.

Dad was not happy with our news. "Why didn't you lock your things in the trunk, out of sight?" he asked.

The whole evening was filled with questions and discussions about what had become of our belongings. We didn't report the theft to the police, but we *did* tell the forest ranger, who said other people had reported missing items in the same area. That night we developed a plan for solving the crime.

The next morning we walked along the road leading to the campground, trying to locate anything the thieves might have discarded on their way back to the main road. After checking the roadsides and finding nothing, we turned back.

That afternoon four determined girls schemed to set a trap for the robbers. The plan was to park the car in the same spot and place valuable items inside — including a purse containing rocks for weight. We would leave the items in plain sight with the windows down for easy access. We informed the ranger of our intentions, and he said he would watch from the hillside across from the parking lot.

At the appointed time, Lois drove my car to the beach with our two younger sisters and two young cousins, who were visiting us at the campground. Cousin Kathy and I arrived in her car. We parked both vehicles, and the younger children went swimming.

The "sleuth sisters" and the older cousins then went into the changing house where we could watch the cars from the highly positioned screened windows. The forest ranger was already in place — with his binoculars in hand.

Within minutes, a young man and woman drove into the parking lot. The man walked toward the picnic table, and the woman approached my car. After looking inside, she gave the man an affirmative nod. She then reached in the window and removed the purse. As she walked toward the man, who was sitting on the picnic table, we dashed out the door of our "changing room position," while the forest ranger ran down from his post. At that moment our mom, dad, and brother Mark, who had been storing bales of hay in the barn, arrived for a swim. Mark's stature as a six-foot-five college football player and the presence of the good-sized forest ranger presented a challenge to the man at the picnic table. He was easily restrained. Someone called the police, and the authorities arrived shortly.

My sister and I were thankful and excited that we were able to solve our own crime with the help of our able cousins. Our local radio station announced: "The state police commend the girls for their actions and bravery." Some months later the criminals were granted their day in court, given the punishment they deserved, and we were able to get back some of our personal items.

As a result of this arrest, other people recovered their stolen belongings and potential future victims were spared the sense of violation we experienced. My sister and I thanked God for his direction and protection. We will never forget our adventurous vacation with a tent — and a purse full of rocks.

. . . .

Those who have been stealing must steal no longer, but must work, doing something useful with their own hands, that they may have something to share with those in need.

EPHESIANS 4:28 TNIV

twins born four years apart

Carol Kent

● ●

A little girl was notified that a baby sister was on the way.
She listened in thoughtful silence, then raised her gaze from her
mother's belly to her eyes and said, "Yes, but who will be
the new baby's mommy?"

JUDITH VIORST

J was an only child for four glorious years. Then Jennie Beth was born. Suddenly my position as the "only" child was usurped by this tiny little bundle of demanding energy that came home from the hospital with my mother and father. It seemed that my mother, who read to me, sang to me, and played games with me had other, more important things to do, and much of her attention revolved around this new member of our household — *my sister!*

Observing my potential for feeling like a "second place" member of the family, my wise mother found creative ways to enlist my help as the "big sister" and gave me important tasks that revolved around caring for my little sister. I ran for diapers, fed her bottles, rocked her, entertained her, and loved her. It didn't take long for me to feel like a significant part of Jennie's life, and a close bond developed. Soon we did everything together and early pictures portray us hand in hand in almost every photograph. We were buddies.

Even though four years separated us in age, we often described each other as "twins" because our interests, hobbies, abilities, and spiritual passions were so similar. We were particularly skilled at finishing each other's sentences, and we had great fun pretending to be the "other" sister when we answered the phone. People couldn't tell our voices apart.

It was no surprise that as preacher's kids with musical ability, we became a duet team. Jennie's clear, sweet soprano tones were a perfect match for my lower alto harmonies. The music brought us great joy and became an integral part of an expanding retreat and conference ministry we enjoyed together.

As the demands of ministry grew more intense, lengthy practices were required for us to add to our musical repertoire and get prepared for ministry commitments. Our *fun* was quickly turning into *hard work*, and all of those practices were more labor intensive than we wanted! Jennie (the more spiritual of the two of us) looked up one day and said, "Carol, when we practice, let's pretend that we are actually singing to God. Let's envision him right here in this room. We'll have an audience of one, but it will be a very important audience."

That suggestion forever changed our attitude toward practice. We were more energized, purposeful, and focused. It reduced any feeling of competition or comparison with each other. It reminded us that ministry is about "him," and not about "us."

Many years have passed since Jennie Beth became my little sister. I'm still flattered when I pick up the phone at her house and people think it's her voice saying "Hello." We still describe ourselves as "twins born four years apart." We both grew up to be speakers and authors, and we are encouraged when people say that our written or spoken ministry has helped them find hope. And the thought that still motivates us and keeps our focus in the right place is the knowledge that we are playing to *an audience of one*!

. . . .

So let's keep focused on that goal, those of us who want everything God has for us. If any of you have something else in mind, something less than total commitment, God will clear your blurred vision — you'll see it yet! Now that we're on the right track, let's stay on it.

PHILIPPIANS 3:15–16 MSG

my sister's handiwork

Bonnie Afman Emmorey

Thank heavens the sun has gone in,
and I don't have to go out and enjoy it.

LOGAN PEARSALL SMITH

"Critically Caucasian." That's what they called me. My husband and I were on a missions trip to the Dominican Republic when that title was first applied by others on our work team. I did look anemic compared to the rest of the population. Somehow the description stuck, even after our return home.

To me it seemed unfair that others around me, even my own family members, could get a tan — and I just burned. I had inherited my grandmother's skin and it did *not* like the sun. My sister Jennie had inherited skin that would not only tan but also glow at every stage in the process. With our completely Dutch ancestry, how could two sisters have such opposite skin?

One year I tried to get a tan. I went boating with my husband and a friend and came home with second-degree burns covering all of my skin that had been exposed to the sun. The doctor was horrified when he saw me in his office the next day. He said he should take pictures for a medical journal because no one would believe him. That day I learned to be very cautious with my skin. No more tanning for me. I had learned my lesson.

Over the years, Jennie and I spent a lot of time at the beach together. My family lived an hour and a half away from where her family vacationed each summer. We drove over for a day trip a couple of times each summer. Of course, Jennie would bask in the sun and enhance her already luscious tan, and I would huddle under the nearest tree, shrub, or umbrella, trying not to expose any flesh.

Jennie would always try to entice me out into the sun, encouraging me to get "just a little." She assured me that it would make me look healthier and less anemic. Since I have been asked if I am an albino, it *was* tempting. But then I would remember my horrible burn, and sanity would return. "No, umm, no, no, I'm really *enjoying* this shady bush." I looked with longing at the rest of the world out playing in the sunshine.

Then came the summer I decided to venture out. Having decided to take a chance and join in the fun, I had purchased some super-powerful sunscreen. I carefully and completely covered every inch of the front half of my body. Then I flipped over and tossed the sunscreen to Jennie. "Could you help me out? Could you cream my legs and back? I *don't* want to get burned!"

"Oh, Bonnie, you will look *great* with a little color," Jennie replied. "Sure, I'll cream you."

That day we had so much fun talking, laughing, and enjoying our time together. Confident I was protected, I stayed out in the sun longer than any other time. What I didn't know was how *little* Jennie actually applied as she lightly glazed her hands over my back and my legs.

That evening we changed out of our bathing suits and into shorts so we could walk into town for ice cream. The kids ran ahead, Jennie and I came next, and our husbands brought up the rear. Our husbands' wild laughter caused us to turn around to find out what was so funny.

My husband Ron hesitantly said, "Honey, are you aware you have white *handprints* on the back of your legs?" Graydon, Jennie's husband, was nodding and laughing.

"*What?*" I craned my head around, trying to see the backs of my legs without any assistance from a mirror. "Jennie, what are they talking about?"

When I looked up and saw the horrified look on Jennie's face, I knew it was true. "Oh, Bonnie, I just tried to apply a *light* coating of sunscreen so you could get a bit more tan. It looks like I might have missed certain areas. Actually, it appears I missed *quite a bit.*"

The backs of my legs were carrying visible proof of the power of sunscreen! It was where Jennie's hands landed with more force that the sunscreen actually "took." My sister's handiwork was clear.

I chose to give up shorts for the rest of the summer because that apparel wasn't worth the laughter it caused. After the handprints *finally* disappeared, I laughed myself. What Jennie did certainly left a mark — but it wasn't permanent. I pray the imprint of Christ on my life is permanent and as visible to those who observe me as my sister's handprints were to our husbands on that hot summer evening.

* * *

Your very lives are a letter that anyone can read by just looking at you. Christ himself wrote it — not with ink, but with God's living Spirit; not chiseled into stone, but carved into human lives — and we publish it.

2 Corinthians 3:2–3 MSG

wedding day blues

Jeanne Zornes

....

A sister is a gift to the heart, a friend to the spirit,
a golden thread to the meaning of life.

ISADORA JAMES

A big red circle on my calendar marked August 15, my wedding day. I was thirty-four and had waited a long time for God's choice of a mate.

My only sibling, my sister Judith, had married at age twenty-nine, ten years earlier. I missed out on her pre-wedding planning because I was working on the other side of the state. I'd flown home the morning of the wedding and watched her put on the gown that Mother had sewn for her.

Mother also sewed the gown for her matron of honor, her college roommate, to match my "used-once" bridesmaid's dress from a friend's wedding earlier that summer.

Mother's sewing abilities always amazed me. My sister and I rarely had a dress, coat, or sports outfit bought at a store because she could sew them for a fraction of the price. But her efforts for my sister's wedding especially touched me when I learned how ill Mother had been with a kidney infection and asthma. She truly wanted to sew her daughter's wedding gown.

Mother always presumed she'd sew my wedding gown too, whenever that time came. One time when I was home, she took me to the cavernous drawers of the hallway linen closet where she kept fabric.

"This is for you, someday," she said, pulling out a large piece of gently folded ivory satin.

But she never got to sew it. When I was thirty-one, she died of cancer. Six months later, my father died of a heart attack.

As my sister and I cleaned out their home, I landed the task of disposing of a sewing room packed with projects and dreams. Neither of us would keep much. Judith rarely sewed. Single and working my way through graduate school, I didn't have much reason to sew.

As I pulled out the fabric-jammed drawer, my fingers ran gently, wistfully, over that creamy expanse of satin. I brushed away some tears as I wrapped it in tissue and put it in the bottom of mother's cedar chest, which I would keep. I hadn't dated anyone seriously in years. I wondered if I'd ever marry.

Then, three years later, I found myself planning my own wedding. With my parents gone, it would be very simple and small. A former roommate offered, as her gift, to sew up that satin in an easy pattern. Another loaned me a veil.

"Just wear a nice dress," I told my sister over the phone as I asked her to be my matron of honor, my only attendant. "And have Christine wear her favorite Sunday outfit." Her nine-year-old daughter would be the flower girl and her seven-year-old son David the ring bearer. If he had his cowlicks tamed, I would be happy. I sewed the ring pillow out of scraps from my dress. My husband-to-be gladly accepted my decision to forsake the tuxedo route and wore a suit instead.

Oh, I'd been to enough weddings to know what brides usually planned. The church would glow with candlelight and baskets of flowers. The bridesmaids and tuxedoed groomsmen would line up with gowns and cummerbunds in a certain color scheme. For me, that would have been blue, my favorite color. Especially a periwinkle blue.

But my heart wasn't in all of that as I came out of my season of grieving. It took all my energies to move from Chicago, where I was working, to the state of Washington, where I'd be married. I couldn't arrange anything fancier — nor could I have afforded it. I knew my sister's family had financial challenges too. A special new dress was one expense they didn't need. And she certainly didn't have the time to sew.

I also felt she didn't need the stress of helping her sister plan a wedding from miles away. We'd already been through too much together in disposing of our parents' things.

There was no wedding rehearsal for this low-budget wedding, so I didn't see my sister until my wedding day at the little country church where my future father-in-law pastored. Roses from a relative's garden filled a couple vases, and a friend had fashioned a bouquet for me out of blue hydrangea blossoms, the closest I got to a blue color scheme.

And then my sister came in with her daughter, in matching peasant-style dresses she had sewn. Of periwinkle satin.

It was the most loving gift she could have given this orphan bride who didn't want to bother anybody. It wasn't just that they matched or were my favorite blue. It was that my sister truly cared to do what our mother might have done.

Wedding over, I came out of the church on the arm of my husband, looked up at the periwinkle sky, and smiled at heaven.

· ·

He has sent me to ... bestow on them ... the oil of gladness
instead of mourning, and a garment of praise
instead of a spirit of despair.

ISAIAH 61:1, 3

the benefits of
having blonde sisters

Carol Kent

. . . .

A blonde went out to her mailbox, looked inside, closed the door of the box, and went back in the house. She repeated this action five times. Her neighbor commented: "You must be expecting a very important letter." The blonde answered, "No, I'm working on my computer, and it keeps telling me I have mail."

FROM *WWW.AHAJOKES.COM*

A couple of years ago, I was speaking at an arena event and realized for the first time in several years, all four of my sisters and my mother would be in the audience. Since I was speaking at a keynote session in front of about six thousand women, I thought it would add variety to the program to have my sisters and my mother on the platform during part of my presentation. I asked each of my sisters to share one thing they learned from our mother that they would pass on to the next generation.

Each sister's response was a tender reminder of our mother's major impact on our lives during our formative years:

- Jennie thanked Mother for being a remarkable story-teller.
- Paula was grateful that Mother helped her make it through a painful divorce, reminding her that Jesus would never leave her.
- Bonnie reminded us that we often saw our mother on her knees and heard her praying out loud for us when we came down the big open staircase in the early morning hours.
- Joy acknowledged that Mother helped her make it through a challenging time in her marriage.
- I told the crowd it was my mother who led me to personal faith in Christ when I was only five years old.

As I looked at my four sisters all standing in a row, it suddenly occurred to me that Jennie was a dark brunette. Paula was a very "highlighted" sunny blonde. Bonnie (a former brunette) was a platinum blonde, Joy's tresses were light brown, and my hair was a vibrant red.

We had all shared serious thoughts, but I thought it was time for a little levity. Scanning the crowd, I said, "I'm sure some of you are wondering how the five of us could have come from the same mother with all these varying shades of color in our hair."

The crowd murmured, and I could hear an audible chuckle. I continued, "Just so you know, except for our mother and my youngest sister, Joy, each of these colors is available to you!" The crowd exploded with laughter.

I (the redhead) will be quick to admit that when I am with either of "the blonde sisters," I always notice they get more attention than I do. When I was younger, I may have been a little jealous, but at this stage of my life, the benefits of having blonde sisters definitely outweigh the negatives. Here are a few reasons why I like hanging out with the blonde sisters:

- We get the best seats in restaurants.
- Strong men immediately help us place our heavy luggage in the overhead compartments on airplanes.
- No one expects us to know the directions to our final destination.
- I don't have the pressure of being the center of attention.
- Other women do not find the non-blonde sisters intimidating.
- I have the privilege of helping people understand that my blonde sisters are actually highly intelligent — which makes me feel extremely valuable!

My four sisters and I are trying to act like mature adults now, but our hair colors are *still* available to you. We figure part of the fun of life is to keep people guessing which of us is the oldest, and we plan to delay "the graying of America" as long as we can hold out.

Since "blondes have more fun," we all plan to end up in the same retirement village someday. However, the main reason we'd like to be together is the bond of sisterhood that connects us at the heart level. We have shared laughter, tears, family crises, graduations, weddings, birthdays, and funerals. And we know that being sisters has strengthened us in a way that goes much deeper than visible "roots."

* *

A cheerful disposition is good for your health;
gloom and doom leave you bone-tired.

PROVERBS 17:22 MSG

my sister's defender

Jill Lynnele Gregory

Sisterhood is a powerful thing.

ROBIN MORGAN

*I*t was one of the most exciting days of my life. My sister was due for delivery. Leanne desperately wanted to be a mom. After struggling through years of infertility, she had finally become pregnant — not with just one baby, but with *two*!

The twins were scheduled for a C-section at thirty-six weeks, but on the day prior to the scheduled surgery, Leanne's blood pressure soared. Following additional blood work, the doctor concluded my sister had a condition known as preeclampsia (hypertension and a buildup of fluid). The C-section needed to be done immediately.

Leanne went into the hospital and all of us experienced sheer exhilaration as she gave birth to two tiny, beautiful baby boys. But moments later our joyful celebration turned into unspeakable fear. Complications set in. Doctors were using unfamiliar terms and my mind was swirling as someone explained that Leanne's organs were shutting down and her life was in danger. Three blood transfusions were given to my sister and we waited for word on her condition. I begged God to let her live.

The turning point in my sister's recovery was the day her husband asked if the twins could be taken out of the neonatal intensive care unit and brought to her. My brother-in-law knew Leanne needed to see the boys so she would have a visual image of why she needed to fight for her life. Soon after that she started sitting up and eventually she was able to walk again. Finally the hospital sent her home, but her twin sons remained in the NICU.

Leanne wanted to bond with her babies and went to the hospital during the feeding times. Normally she would show her sons' ID bracelets on her wrists and the guard would allow her to pass the security desk and go directly to the elevator. Since she did this on a daily basis, the guards knew her and just waved her past the security checkpoint.

Leanne was still very frail one day when I helped her enter the hospital. A guard I had never seen before stopped her from his seat behind a high counter. Leanne looked up and showed him the ID bracelets and explained that she was at the hospital to feed her twins. He flashed her a mean look and told her she was not allowed past him without a hospital pass. She explained that she had never had to get a hospital pass before and had been instructed to show the twins' ID bracelets when she needed to get in to feed her babies.

He glared down at her from his powerful perch and said with disgust, "I don't care what you've done in the past. You'll have to go down the hall and get a hospital pass today!"

My sister was very weak, but managed a reply. "Yes, but sir, I've never needed a pass, just the twins' ID bracelets — "

Before she could finish her sentence, the guard blurted out angrily, "*I don't care what you've done before! Get a pass!*" Then, with a smug look on his face, he did one of those rolling wrist gestures that ended with a finger pointing to the nurse's station down the hall. Leanne was flustered and upset. So was I.

I was born a redhead and my feisty spirit has remained strong. The anger that arose in me as I observed this man demean my sister in her exhausted and weakened state is hard to describe. His demeanor was nothing short of cruel.

My sister slowly turned and shuffled down the hall with tears in her eyes. I stopped her.

"No, Leanne, you sit here. You are in no shape to run through this hospital to get a pass. I'll get it." I sat her down in a chair and walked to the end of the hall to the nurse's station.

I fumed as I waited. When my turn came, I inquired, "Excuse me. Does my sister need a pass to feed her children today?"

The nurse looked over, saw Leanne, and immediately waved to her. "No, she's fine. She can go right up to the neonatal intensive care unit."

Pointing my finger down the hall, I said, "That guard won't let her through." The guard with the "attitude" glared back at me.

The nurse shouted down the long hallway, "Hey! Let her through. She's okay."

As I stormed back down the hall, the guard approached my sister. Suddenly words came out of my mouth that surprised me: "Don't you talk to her! Leave her alone!" I grabbed Leanne and tried to shield her from the cold-hearted guard.

He started backpedaling, "Hey, look, I was only doing my job, and I don't usually work this post."

"Sir," I said, "that gives you no right to talk to someone in such a demeaning way."

I ushered Leanne into the elevator. As we made our way up several floors, my sister had tears in her eyes. "Thank you," she said softly. "That guard was so mean. I just didn't have the strength to fight him." Then she said with a smile, "I have never seen you so angry. You are really scary when you're that upset." We hugged and realized we could finally laugh out loud as we slowly made our way to the twins.

Several years have passed since I protected Leanne in that hospital corridor. I still love "being there" for her when she needs me, and I know she'll do the same for me when the tables are turned. After all, we're sisters!

* *

Jonathan was deeply impressed with David — an immediate bond was forged between them. He became totally committed to David. From that point on he would be David's number-one advocate and friend.

1 Samuel 18:1 MSG

a memorable road trip

Bonnie Afman Emmorey

* *

*Laughter need not be cut out of anything,
since it improves everything.*

JAMES THURBER

*J*t was a bitterly cold night. My sister Carol and I were on our way home from teaching a seminar in Indianapolis, and we had a very long road trip ahead of us. The drive started out normally enough, but the farther we traveled, the more we needed to do creative brainstorming to make the miles go by more quickly.

Somehow we ended up on the subject of death, and while ordinarily it's not a humorous subject, that night we were just tired enough to find the laughter in this usually somber theme. I could just picture Carol being fitted for her heavenly gown and her angelic wings.

We decided to use the next hour to plan our own funerals. To some that may seem morbid, but since Carol and I are ready to face eternity with joy and our family *loves* a gathering of any sort, planning our home-going celebrations seemed like an appropriate use of our time on this long trek home.

With laughter punctuating every idea, we made lists of favorite family foods that could be served, and we decided the event definitely called for great music. We figured if the family was getting together anyway, they might as well have a fabulous meal and extraordinary entertainment. Our exhaustion added to the combined hilarity and absurdity of the moment.

Suddenly Carol quit laughing and took me by surprise as she paused a moment and very seriously asked, "Bonnie, if I go first, will you do my eulogy?"

Her sincere demeanor stunned me momentarily, and I came face to face with a fact of my life. I lose control at funerals. I might not even know the deceased personally, but show me a dead body in a box, and I go to pieces. Totally out of control.

Because Carol is not just my sister but also one of my all-time favorite people, I was honored to think that she wanted *me* to do her eulogy. But I had a disturbing vision of me at that memorial service — bulbous red nose streaming, tissue box in hand, hiccupping erratically as I tried to speak.

It was clear to me that she was having difficulty understanding my dilemma. This is a woman who has made "being appropriate" a fine art. It would be difficult to find a more politically correct, perfectly coiffured, classically dressed, and poised-at-all-times woman. The image of my blotched face and tattered tissues returned.

However, within moments, Carol came up with the perfect solution and she blurted out, "You could do lip-synching!" She suggested I tape the audio ahead of time and just move my lips during the service. We howled with laughter. Carol thought people would be touched by my emotion because tears are very appropriate at a funeral. She could picture it all — my voice speaking eloquently while I dabbed a tear from the corner of my eye. Her beautiful, tasteful picture of this event and my nightmarish version were not even close!

That night we laughed until we cried, and I realized anew how blessed I am to have a sister like Carol.

Since memorial services are technically for the ones left behind, I've decided to start a new tradition — a *living* eulogy. That way Carol can know what I'll be lip-synching at her service.

Carol, you are a rare and beautiful woman. Your inner beauty is as vivid as your outer shell, and the combination is a two-part harmony that fills any room with sweet music. People are drawn to you because of your "calm and gentle spirit, a thing very precious in the eyes of God" (1 Peter 3:4 Phillips).

Many people will be in the kingdom of heaven because you wisely used the gifts you were given. Not only did you use your own gifts, you multiplied them as you trained others in ministry. Your words are as "apples of gold in settings of silver" (Proverbs 25:11).

You are my beloved sister. You make family reunions a celebration. You are my dear friend. You know how to keep a secret. You are my beloved mentor. No one could be a more Christlike woman. I love you.

Our road trip finally came to an end. We had laughed hard and we loved much. I am sadly aware that there is no way I could ever make it through my sister's eulogy — even lip-synching.

So here's the deal, Carol. I'll go first and you can do *my* eulogy. No, wait a minute. Let's go together and have the great joy of hearing our welcome-home greetings from our Lord himself.

• •

Now there is in store for me the crown of righteousness, which the Lord, the righteous Judge, will award to me on that day — and not only to me, but also to all who have longed for his appearing.

2 TIMOTHY 4:8

sistah! sistah!

Toni Schirico Horras

. . . .

Sisters function as safety nets in a chaotic world
simply by being there for each other.

CAROL SALINE

My sisters and I were busy assembling dinner in the church kitchen when the overhead speaker indicated the worship music had ended in the sanctuary and the pastor was about to lead the congregation in a time of prayer. My sisters stopped in the middle of their work and looked in my direction.

One precious friend spoke up: "Pastor is going to pray for Jared today. Let's stop our work and pray too." We found each other's hands and stood in a circle. I realized in that moment I had been trying to bury my pain by staying busy. Helping to prepare for this dinner kept the focus off my aching heart. One by one I listened as these "closer-than-family" sisters prayed for me and for my wayward son.

When my husband and I first adopted transracially over seventeen years ago, I began to pray for friends of color. I wanted girlfriends, sisters, sistahs! I wanted peers to help me understand what I couldn't possibly comprehend growing up in my white skin. I wanted to be confronted when I was wrong and set straight. I didn't want my two adopted African-American sons to be disadvantaged because they had a Caucasian mother.

It was a bold and ignorant prayer. But over time God answered. Some of my prayed-for friends were in that kitchen; many were in other parts of the church, and others were scattered across the country. In many settings, I look around and suddenly realize I am the only white woman present. My caller ID list is frequently all friends of color. One of my dear friends nicknamed me "Sistah-girl." A close friend who regards me as a blood sister once caught herself saying, "Oh, yeah, I forgot for a minute that you are white." What a compliment! I chuckled one day as my friends of color got together and told me I "passed"!

Each one understands my heartache too well. Many are grandmas; some are my age and grandmas many times over. One woman has watched her brother live a playboy's life, father a child, and still "act a fool." Another had a son leave home for weeks only to wake up one wintry morning to find him curled up asleep on her front stoop — repentant and hungry. Many have sons in prison; one has had two incarcerated sons at once.

Another has a daughter on her third child out of wedlock — and my dear sister loves those babies with all her might. Several have sons lost to the streets — whereabouts unknown. And yet another has a son who was murdered. She wears a locket around her neck with his picture inside. Others blessedly have sons who love God with all their hearts and have not succumbed to temptation.

These were the sisters who felt my pain and loved me enough to boldly beseech God's throne for me that day. I could tell by how they prayed they had "been there" for their own loved ones many times. Tears flowed. How immensely good of God to surround me with this depth of understanding! How silly of me to think I would be spared this pain when none of them had been. How could I have thought I would sidestep this trial when each of their sons and brothers had to face all the same temptations my son had. How high and mighty of me to ever think I might escape this burden!

When I first asked God for friends of color, I thought it was to benefit my sons. And it has — but not nearly as much as it has benefited me. How like God to draw us into something that makes sense to our human way of thinking and then turn it completely around to teach us things he wants us to learn.

And that is just what is happening with my wayward son. He thinks he is running away from us and away from all things white and middle class to authentic blackness. He thinks the restlessness he feels is because he is not really "black enough."

He attributes the angst that weighs him down to his adoption and being "taken away from his people."

When will he come home, look around, and see these loving, generous, and godly people he rejected? I have no idea when the lightbulb will go on in his mind and heart, but I pray he'll come home soon and make up for lost time. I long to experience the years the locusts have eaten. I wasn't finished with mothering this son. Meanwhile, I will trust God and lean on the support of my knowledgeable, experienced "been there, done that" sistahs!

Let perseverance finish its work so that you may be mature and complete, not lacking anything. If any of you lacks wisdom, you should ask God, who gives generously to all without finding fault, and it will be given to you.

JAMES 1:4 – 5 TNIV

a cherished treasure

Shirley Carter Liechty

....

Duty makes us do things well,
but love makes us do them beautifully.

PHILLIPS BROOKS

*A*s I rode the bus to school that day, a lone tear stung my cheek, and I stared out the window in silence. My face flushed and my heart pounding, my mind was going in many different directions. I was anxious and upset — fearful of being ridiculed by classmates once they learned my secret. My best friend, Sarah, met me outside the school. As our eyes met, she knew something was terribly wrong. I burst into tears and exploded with my announcement, "My mom is going to have *another* baby."

However, my anticipation of embarrassment over having my peers discover my parents were still engaged in enlarging our family (which already numbered six) was very short-lived. Sarah's enthusiasm about the coming baby was contagious, and she soon had several of my fellow students and a favorite teacher involved in planning a baby shower for my new sibling. It didn't take long for my concerns about what others thought of my family to disappear. The excitement and attention made the prospects of becoming a big sister again enjoyable and fun.

My beautiful new sister was born in mid-March, and my mother surprised me by allowing me to choose her name. I called her Marcia Ellen. Two months later I celebrated my eighteenth birthday, and just two weeks after that I graduated from high school.

The summer went by quickly, and I began my first semester of college in northeastern Indiana. As a freshman at a conservative Christian school, I wasn't officially allowed to leave the campus for a return trip home until Thanksgiving weekend. Although I enjoyed classes, making friends, and adjusting to being on my own, I also missed my family. By November, I was ready for a break from school, and I was more than eager to get home and see my growing baby sister.

Being home again was wonderful! On this holiday weekend our family of seven, plus my grandmother, packed into our 1955 Mercury for a one-day visit at Aunt Ruby and Uncle Red's house. Their country home was charming and the expansive property was complete with a stream, woods, and a pond — and Aunt Ruby was an incredible cook!

After the first forty miles, Dad pulled into a gas station. Looking over his shoulder into the backseat, he noticed that almost everyone had fallen asleep. Immediately suspecting a leak in the exhaust system, he began evacuating the family from the vehicle. The fumes hadn't affected my father or the other front-seat passengers (Grandma and me) because along the way he had opened the driver's window vent. As the doors were flung open, my brother exited the car and fell, nearly striking his head on the cement near the gas pumps. Service station attendants telephoned for help.

I noticed my mother was dazed and appeared to be in shock. I pulled back the baby blanket and looked at Marcia. I was horrified when I saw my baby sister's face. She was blue-gray in color, very cool, motionless, and her eyes were rolled back in her head. I took her from my mother's arms and quickly asked for God to help me. I immediately remembered one of my classmates presenting a current events report on a new life-saving technique. Rather than doing nothing, my instinctive response was to at least try this new procedure. Laying Marcia down, I carefully placed my mouth over hers and I began mouth-to-mouth resuscitation.

For the next few moments, time stood still. Then, finally, Marcia took a breath and began to cry. Moments later the neighborhood fire department rescue unit arrived. They checked all of us and, after hearing the story of what transpired, one of the officers said, "That baby's big sister no doubt saved her life!" The color had come back into Marcia Ellen's face, and I breathed a huge sigh of relief.

Dad checked the car thoroughly and discovered the exhaust pipe had become plugged with mud when the car had been driven off the road into a ditch earlier in the week. Now certain it was safe, we all climbed back into the car and resumed our trip. My dad wept on and off for most of the rest of the day, reminding us of how much he loved us and telling us just how *special* this Thanksgiving really was!

Thoughts were swirling in my mind. I was horrified the previous year when Mom found out she was going to have a baby. But the very thing I thought was going to be a major embarrassment turned out to be one of my greatest joys — the birth of Marcia Ellen. I breathed deeply and sighed, realizing that I had not only been given the privilege of naming my baby sister — God had allowed me to save her life. Although we would always be separated by years, she had become a cherished treasure, and I knew that I loved her dearly.

．．

Love never gives up. . . . Love cares more for others than for self.
. . . isn't always "me first," . . . trusts God always . . .
keeps going to the end.

SELECTIONS FROM 1 CORINTHIANS 13:4–7 MSG

diaper service

Elizabeth Murphy

· ·

How do people make it through life without a sister?

SARA CORPENING

*I*t was Saturday night in Cleveland, Ohio, as I sat alone in the hospital with my new baby and my mixed emotions. I was overjoyed at the miracle of birth and the precious little boy who slept in my arms. I was overwhelmed at the thought of taking him home to his thirteen-month-old brother and his busy dad, who spent lots of time traveling for work. Mostly, I was overcome with loneliness and the deep emptiness that comes from not being able to share the truly important moments in life with those you love.

Mike and I had transferred from Raleigh, North Carolina, to a home in Cleveland only two months before Andrew's birth. In the brief time we had lived there, my life was more than busy: I lived in a hotel for a month with a one-year-old and two big Labrador retrievers, moved into an old house that needed a makeover, sent my husband on countless business trips, and dealt with finding doctors, hairstylists, banks, babysitters, and grocery stores in a new city. I had no time to make new friends.

Then came news that my younger sister Susan, only four weeks postpartum after giving birth to her fourth son, had been diagnosed with cancer. My extended family went into a panicked overdrive trying to figure out how to care for my sister. She was in Dallas — and I was *very pregnant* in Cleveland. The focus needed to be on Susan, but I had never felt so helpless, alone, and far from home.

The real estate agent who sold us our house lived in the same area we did and had a daughter of babysitting age. She was the first one we called when I went into labor and had to leave for the hospital. There was literally no one else to watch our one-year-old.

In the midst of Susan's sickness, the birth of our precious Andrew was a bright spot, but one that could only be celebrated with phone calls and sweet words via long distance. My heart ached for so much more.

As I settled in for the good long cry I knew I deserved, I heard a knock on the door and the sound of robust giggles. I couldn't imagine who it could be. I didn't know anyone in Cleveland besides my husband who would visit me in the hospital.

The door opened. It was Joan, my realtor, followed by her three young daughters. The girls were so excited to see a brand-new baby, they literally *fell* into my room, filling the space with enthusiasm, joy, and exuberance. They carried a huge package of baby-boy diapers, tied with an equally large bundle of balloons — the biggest and brightest kind.

"We couldn't stay away," Joan said, "but we didn't know if it was okay to come either. Your sister, Amy, gave us the perfect excuse. Here!" she said as she handed me a card.

My older sister Amy had tracked down the only person I knew in Cleveland — my realtor — and asked her to buy the diapers and balloons and personally deliver them to me in the hospital. The card said:

Welcome, Baby Andrew!

Sorry we can't be with you, but we will be so excited to meet you and welcome you to the family. We love you, your mom, dad, and brother, too.

Love,
Aunt Amy

No gift could have pleased me more. It wasn't just the package. My room was filled with beautiful flowers from lots of loved ones. It was the presence of a person that touched me so.

Amy knew, in the way only a sister cut from the same cloth could know, that as bad as I felt about Susan's illness, and as much as I knew she needed all of our family to rally around her, I needed them too. She sent me so much more than a present —

she sent me a person. That day I was reminded that our creative God sometimes uses realtors, balloons, diapers, and sisters who are far away to remind us of his love and to lift our heads when we are discouraged, lonely, or downhearted.

But you are a shield around me, O Lord; you bestow glory on me and lift up my head.

PSALM 3:3

the shopping divas

Bonnie Afman Emmorey

···

Sisters are girlfriends, rivals, listening posts, shopping buddies,
confidantes, and so much more.

CAROL SALINE

*T*he Afman girls have many similarities — and one
thing we all enjoy is shopping. My sister Jennie
and I are probably the most alike in our technique. We both consider shopping to be our best sport and we
are competitive.

A few years ago, the two of us were in San Diego for a seminar, and we decided to stay an extra day so we could do some
shopping in Tijuana, Mexico. We knew it would be an unusual
escapade, but we had no idea just how much adventure awaited
us on the following day.

We started out bright and early as we mentally prepared for
"wheeling and dealing" with the locals. Jennie and I jumped
on a train near our hotel and got off when the conductor
announced that we were at the border crossing. Then we faced

our first problem. *We couldn't find Mexico!* We expected signs or at least something indicating we were coming to the end of one country and were entering another. How could we "run to the border" if we couldn't even find it?

We must have looked bewildered because a man walked over and asked if we needed any help. We asked him to point us in the direction of the Mexican border, and he said, "Follow me. I'm going that way myself."

The man was *totally* dressed in black leather, with shoulder-length stringy hair, and he was smoking something. This was not a guy I would feel comfortable following anywhere, certainly not into a foreign country. But before I could say a word, my sister sincerely thanked him, fell into step beside him, and struck up a conversation.

Since I knew we had to stick together, I brought up the rear. We followed him down a walkway and through a turnstile. That was it! He told us we were now in Mexico. There were no border guards or customs officials.

I was trying to gently pry Jennie away from the fellow in the black leather, but it was not working. I overheard him say, "How would you like to see the *real* Mexico?"

I was thinking, "*Are you kidding?*" But before I could protest, I heard my sister respond with an affirmative word, and once again I realized I couldn't leave her, so I simply followed along.

He took us to an old bus that was stuffed with people and their livestock. It cost thirty-five cents for the ride, and it was straight out of the movie *Romancing the Stone*. My seat was next to a woman and her pig. I tried hard to lean *away* from the aroma. The air was so foul I could hardly breathe. I had visions of being abducted and sold into white slavery and my husband and sons hearing about it on the evening news.

Jennie was still conversing politely with her newfound friend and had even progressed to showing him pictures of her family. I shot visual warning daggers in her direction.

In spite of my fears, the man in black turned out to be a kind person who gave us excellent advice. He helped us get off at a bus stop in downtown Tijuana, suggested where we should go and where *not* to go, and gave us instructions regarding what to offer a cab driver for the ride back to the border.

That day two sisters made choices that could have landed them in serious trouble. However, in spite of our uncertain circumstances, Jennie and I enjoyed a glorious day of shopping. We perfected the art of bartering and bought sombreros and ponchos for our kids.

We seriously considered keeping the events of the day to ourselves — but decided it might be better to tell our families and use our impulsive actions as a lesson in what *not* to do. We knew God had spared us from potential danger and we should have sought wise counsel *before* entering a foreign country.

. . . .

Without good direction, people lose their way; the more wise counsel you follow, the better your chances.

PROVERBS 11:14 MSG

the "healing" quilt

Anne Denmark

The only true gift is a portion of yourself.

EMERSON

*a*t 4:45 p.m. on February 1, 2003, I was crushed between life and death, wondering if I would ever take another breath. It was my husband Don's fifty-second birthday. To celebrate we had flown to Muncie, Indiana, to participate in Parents' Weekend for the Ball State University volleyball team. Our son was a senior on the team and we had just left the luncheon banquet with Matthew and the student trainer, Mike, when a truck struck our rental car from behind. The first impact crushed my back and my scapula, clavicle, sternum, and ribs. Our car then veered into oncoming traffic and collided with an SUV, breaking Don's shoulder and pinning his leg under the dashboard. Matthew and Mike were able to get out of the car and get help.

Our birthday celebration turned into an all-night visit to the emergency room and, ultimately, into a time of prayerful thanksgiving for spared lives. For me, that evening was also the beginning of an eleven-day hospital stay and months of painful recovery, which required me to wear a restricting back brace and bone stimulator.

The injuries put frustrating limits on my active life. Each morning I would wake to another day totally reliant on others to bathe, dress, and roll me into the body brace. It was humbling to be so helpless. It was humbling to need so much help. Day after day my only job was to wait and heal. Sometimes the hours of pain chipped away at me until discouragement clouded my thoughts. *Would I ever get better?*

News of our accident resulted in an unbelievable outpouring of long-distance love from Don's mother and three sisters. Several weeks after returning to our home in Oklahoma, a large box containing a handmade quilt arrived at our door. As I unfolded the gift, a cheerful array of color spilled over my lap. Tucked inside was a letter from my sister-in-law Kathy sharing the story behind the quilt. It began with her prayer, and I read it through tears of joy.

> "Lord, my sister-in-law is hurting, and I want her to know how much she is loved. It's so hard to be so far away — to feel so helpless."
>
> Make her a quilt.
>
> "A quilt, Lord? But I'm just a beginner . . ."
>
> A quilt, Kathy. Others will help.

For Kathy the prompting came immediately, and she called Louise and Janet and Mom. They all wanted to be a part of the quilt. Without hesitation their sewing machines came out, and the rest of the day all three of them, at the same time, were stitching their prayers and love into squares for me. I could picture each of them in their homes. They lived so far apart yet remained so close in purpose through this flurry of activity.

They decided to make a charm quilt. No two squares of fabric were supposed to be the same. Each of them made six large squares by sewing sixteen smaller squares together, portraying their personalities in the choice of fabrics. Funny thing though, six of Lou's squares and six of Kathy's squares were made of the same fabric. They had even sewn two of the same squares side-by-side. Jan and Kathy had two squares the same also. Later I would run my fingers over the squares trying to figure out which sister chose which squares.

Kathy knew my passion for flowers and gardening so she chose the floral fabric for the borders. Its brilliant blue holds a profusion of white daisies anchored with their yellow centers. You can't help but smile when you see those sunshine colors.

When it was time to quilt, Kathy said; "I wanted the best for you." She knew a woman who was kind enough to put aside other quilts and professionally quilt their project in a timely manner. The daisies on the border print were replicated with her fine stitches and far exceeded even Kathy's expectations.

Sewing down the binding was Kathy's favorite stitching to do so she did that herself because she said; "It is so therapeutic."

Naming of the quilt was a combined effort. Jan knew "Jehovah-Rapha" meant the Lord's name for healing. Lou chose the name of the quilt — "Healing." Mom chose the Scripture, Exodus 15:26, "I am the Lord that heals you." These words were beautifully embroidered on a label and inserted on the back corner. They all chose not to put their names on the quilt because I would know who it was from.

I smiled as I read the closing words in the letter. "This quilt is for you, Anne. It is sent with so much love, so much prayer, so much encouragement and so much hope. Don might ask, "Where is my quilt?" We're hoping you get better so quickly that he can snuggle closely with you under this one! We love you!"

I wrapped myself up in the comfort of the healing quilt and snuggled deep into their love. I was humbled to think of the incredible tenderness of my Heavenly Father. He brought the hearts and hands of my sisters together to cover me with long-distance love. The healing had begun.

* *

Praise be to the God and Father of our Lord Jesus Christ, the Father of compassion and the God of all comfort, who comforts us in all our troubles.

2 CORINTHIANS 1:3 – 4

two lives — one heartbeat

Charlotte Adelsperger

*M*y mother's pregnancy held a mystery in the late 1930s. With no sonograms or high-tech blood tests, all she could announce was, "It's a *big* baby." In her eighth month she told her doctor, "It feels like an octopus — limbs moving in every direction! Could there be more than one?"

"Be assured, Mary, there's only one baby," Dr. Vaughn said, lifting his stethoscope from her abdomen. "I get one strong heartbeat." She took him at his word and continued to cover her unborn child with tender prayers.

But surprise! Mother's early labor brought the arrival of twin girls! Our prenatal heartbeats had been synchronized. She and my father were thrilled even though we were not well and needed much medical care. Our parents gave us the feminine forms of our grandfathers' names. I, the firstborn, became

Charlotte named for Charles, and my twin was named Alberta for Albert.

As identical twins we teamed up to respond to the questions of curious people. By age ten, we had a ready answer when anyone asked, "Are you two twins?"

"Yes, *both* of us," I'd say, a little flippantly.

Throughout childhood, we forsook any sibling competition and consistently rejoiced in each other's accomplishments. One of us would run to tell our parents how well the other did at school. "It's so much fun having a twin sister!" we'd say.

During our teen years, Alberta and I stepped into a rich adventure. We both deepened in our love for the Lord and made individual commitments to Christ. We became steady prayer partners, sharing everything. We had an optimistic outlook and a mutual love for people. Together we began to strive to live up to what the apostle Paul taught, "Sing and make music in your heart to the Lord, always giving thanks to God the Father for everything, in the name of our Lord Jesus Christ" (Ephesians 5:19–20).

Alberta married first, and we continued in closeness and in prayer. I'll never forget the June when her baby was overdue. I was at a church institute at campgrounds in the Black Hills of South Dakota. She was in Charleston, South Carolina.

One night as I slept in the women's tent, I kept waking up and praying for Alberta. By early morning I was vigorously sweeping the tent floor.

"Charlotte, *what* are you doing?" one of the young women asked.

"Can't explain it — I think my sister is in labor. Just a feeling. Let's pray for Alberta." Several women joined me in prayer.

By mid-morning I got a telegram from Charleston. Alberta had given birth to a healthy baby boy! Yes, she had been in labor during those very hours when I had an urgency to pray for her. I headed up to the hills by myself and sang Alberta's favorite hymn at the top of my lungs. "Praise to the Lord, the Almighty, the King of creation!"

Years later when I was in labor for my first baby, Alberta had a similar nudge from the Lord. She prayed and, on hands and knees, vigorously scrubbed her kitchen floor! She was "tuned in," for sure. Soon after, the phone call came announcing my baby girl.

"We're best friends from birth," Alberta remarks. "And we pray earnestly for each other's needs when they arise."

"We have many stories of how God has answered our prayers," I add.

We're twins with individual gifts, but through our closeness in Christ, we will always have one heartbeat.

....

Do not be anxious about anything, but in everything, by prayer and petition, with thanksgiving, present your requests to God. And the peace of God, which transcends all understanding, will guard your hearts and your minds in Christ Jesus.

PHILIPPIANS 4:6–7

bunny hill sunshine

Jennie Afman Dimkoff

· ·

Seize the day!

HORACE

*T*hat *does* sounds like fun, Carol. The kids would love it. All right, we'll go!" I couldn't resist my sister Carol, who was using her considerable motivational skill to convince me that a ski trip would be a great way for our families to spend time together. Hanging up, I stared at the phone. What had I committed myself to? The last time I'd gone skiing was in high school, when I'd come home with a sprained ankle after crashing into the lodge.

In preparation for the trip, I went outlet-mall shopping, buying our entire family ski pants. For myself, I purchased a lovely ensemble in teal, black, and fuchsia. I knew Carol's ski suit was light turquoise, and we would coordinate beautifully. (I was certain that *looking* like a skier was the first step to *being* a skier.)

Upon checking in at the resort, we decided to make reservations for dinner at seven and take advantage of the beautiful, sunny afternoon to go cross-country skiing. "It really is easy," Carol assured me, "and we'll be able to talk all along the way."

There were six of us when we started out. Carol's son had opted for hitting the daredevil downhill slopes, but our husbands and my two children were with us. Caught up in conversation, Carol and I fell to the rear of the group, taking our time. A natural encourager, Carol was drawing me out about recent ministry experiences, and our time together was precious to me.

An hour later, the kids announced that they were going on ahead, so we waved good-bye and fell back into deep conversation. Reaching the point where we thought the kids had turned, we suddenly realized our husbands were out of sight as well. Calling out to no avail, we decided to take a shortcut back to the lodge. My muscles were already screaming, and I was longing for a hot bath before dinner.

Five hours later, we still had not reached the lodge, and I knew it would be dark soon. I was close to tears, and Carol's "I don't understand how we managed to get so *far* from civilization" comment was no comfort. I had taken off my skis two hours earlier and was lugging the expensive rental property, sorely tempted to throw it aside as I stumbled along. "Downhill skiing is much easier than this, Jennie," Carol assured me. "I'm amazed that this trail is so rough and uneven."

She had no sooner made that comment when I noticed a marker along the trail. "Carol, what does that black diamond shape on that sign mean?"

We were lost on the roughest trail we could have chosen! "I want to just lie down and sleep for a while," I whined. Carol insisted that we keep going.

The sunset was beautiful, but I missed its majesty, thinking only of impending nightfall and the fact that the temperature was dropping rapidly. Coming to a halt, Carol turned toward me, her breath emerging in frosty puffs in the freezing air. "I think we should pray, Jennie. God knows where we are, even if we don't."

Two colorful amateur skiers bowed their heads and pleaded with God for help.

"Helloooo!" Lifting our heads and turning in the direction of the voice, we saw a lone skier, waving at us. Certain our prayers had been answered immediately, we waved back wildly, only to be disappointed. Although he was a far better skier than we were, he was lost too, and he was rapidly dehydrating. Still, his presence was a comfort.

We managed to climb a steep embankment to a beautiful house, but we banged repeatedly on the door to no avail. We actually considered breaking a window of the luxurious place, sure that a burglar alarm would go off and we would be rescued, but the thought of vandalism charges held us back. The house seemed to be on a narrow deserted lane, and having no idea where it led, we decided to get back on the ski trail, certain that it would lead to the lodge and our husbands, *who should have been out looking for us*!

In the fading light we finally spotted a large house on a hill in the distance. Our spirits rose as we climbed the embankment and saw vehicles lining the driveway. The homeowner was not gracious, but begrudgingly let us use the phone. One of her guests offered to drive us to the lodge several miles away, where our very worried husbands met us with open arms. They hurried to notify the ski patrol that we were back.

The next morning I awoke with a painful groan to the ringing of the phone. "Good morning, dear sister!" sang Carol. "I've signed us up for beginner lessons on the bunny hill. Meet me for breakfast in thirty minutes and we'll hit the slopes at ten!"

Sister Sunshine had lovingly motivated me once again.

* *

Gently encourage the stragglers, and reach out for the exhausted, pulling them to their feet. Be patient with each person, attentive to individual needs.

1 THESSALONIANS 5:14 MSG

a matter of perspective

Bonnie Afman Emmorey

· ·

If you judge people, you have no time to love them.

MOTHER TERESA

*J*t was December and the family was coming to my house for the holiday celebration. Little did I know that something important, even life-changing, was going to happen to me during that reunion.

The event took place on the day after Christmas. My mother, two of my sisters, and I decided to go into town to the coffee shop where we planned to meet our husbands later. The guys, all bundled up in their winter gear, were running to town through the woods behind our house, but we drove the three miles to town. Mother, Carol, Jennie, and I sat in one booth chatting over our coffee and tea, eating delicious peanut butter cinnamon rolls, while the guys took over another section of the restaurant. We laughed and chatted, savoring our time together, knowing that before long everyone would be headed for their various homes.

We left Joy, our youngest sister and the main topic of our discussion, home playing with the nieces and nephews. Joy was in her late teens — beautiful, talented, intelligent, and very much pursued by the male gender. That morning, we were discussing all of her beaus, listing their positive virtues, or their lack of admirable traits, and generally evaluating which boyfriend we thought would fit into our family best.

One particular name came up, and I burst in with my evaluation. "He's *so egotistical*." Unfortunately, I had never even met the man, but I was putting him down based on something I had once heard someone say.

Quietly, from beside me, I heard my sister Jennie say, "Well, he *does* have a healthy self-esteem."

My heart was pierced!

We had basically said the same thing, just from opposite perspectives — negative and positive. The conversation continued on to the next prospective boyfriend. No one there was aware of it, but I had just encountered one of those soul-baring moments. I knew it wasn't the only time I had chosen a judgmental word over an affirming word.

It was frightening to me as I realized that I had allowed myself to slowly sink into being a negative, critical person. At that time, my sons were young, and I knew that my example would shape their opinions and attitudes. I was the pattern they observed daily.

After my sisters and their families left that day, I faced my problem. I had been choosing to live in a negative world when

I didn't have to. The choice was mine. I knew that my perspective was just that — a perspective. My husband Ron and I had often laughed about that very thing. I once made the comment that his sports car "drove like a truck." Ron said, "No, you can *feel* the road!" Same thing — different perspective. Positive versus negative. I knew I had a decision to make. It was time to quit living in a negative world.

I prayed and told God that I wanted to trade in my old negative attitude for a positive one. I wanted to learn to see the good in every situation, to be a builder of people, not a destroyer. That day in the coffee shop, my sister set an example for me that forever changed my perspective.

. . . .

Do not let any unwholesome talk come out of your mouths, but only what is helpful for building others up according to their needs, that it may benefit those who listen.

EPHESIANS 4:29

the color of sunshine

Carol Kent

· ·

A sister hears your heart before a word is spoken.
A sister tastes your tears, and feels your joy.

DEBORAH LINDSAY O'TOOLE

*I*t had been the worst experience of my life. My boat had been rocked. My confidence had eroded. I questioned my worth as a mother, a wife, a sister, a friend. If I could have curled up in the embryo position, fallen asleep, and said good-bye to life, that would have been my choice. No, I wasn't actually suicidal. I just didn't think there was much about life that made it worth living.

My husband and I had received the devastating news that our son, a graduate of the U.S. Naval Academy, had been arrested for a heinous crime. The details surrounding this bizarre and shocking announcement took my breath away and put me into a deep depression. (I've told the full story in my book *When I Lay My Isaac Down*.)

Most of us have had a phone call, a diagnosis from a doctor, a financial reversal, a betrayal by a loved one, or a crisis in life that made us question God's love for us, our value to others, and our ability to go on with a normal life. That was me. I felt like standing up and saying, "I quit life! It's too hard! It's too unfair! I don't have the energy to fight anymore! I'm disappointed in God! I give up!"

In the middle of my depression and despair, the doorbell rang. It was a deliveryman with a large covered object in his hand. With a cheery smile, he said, "Are you Carol Kent?"

I nodded.

"Well, it's your lucky day! Somebody must want to make you feel special today, and I have the privilege of delivering this gift. Enjoy your day!"

He disappeared as quickly as he came, and I found myself holding the covered object in my hands. It was enveloped in green florist paper. I took it to the island in the middle of my kitchen. As I tore away the protective covering, my eyes fell on one dozen of the most perfect yellow roses I had ever laid eyes on.

I carefully opened the sealed envelope, and the note took me by surprise. It was from two of my sisters. It read:

Dear Carol,

You once gave us some decorating advice that was very helpful. You said, "Yellow flowers will brighten any room." We thought you could use a little yellow in your life right now.

Love,
Bonnie and Joy

At that moment the skylight over my kitchen island revealed glorious sunshine pouring its rays on my beautiful bouquet. The yellow roses glistened in between the baby's breath and soft green fern, bringing an artistic glow to the unexpected gift.

Tears flooded my eyes and I heard myself wailing like a mother mourning a great loss. I hadn't realized until that moment, that I hadn't given myself permission to grieve over my deep disappointment or to express my feelings out loud. I had been slapping on a fake smile, being strong for others, and masking my heavy heart. It was a moment of honest grief and, for the first time in a long time, I felt like my life had a new degree of authenticity.

From that day on, yellow was my color of hope. My sisters sent yellow cards, yellow candles, and yellow packages. And they spread the word. Friends and other family members picked up on using the color of sunshine — yellow — to remind me that no matter what happens to us, no matter who disappoints us, no matter what crisis crosses our path, we can always find hope.

My sisters were right, even though they were reminding me of my own advice. Yellow flowers *will* brighten any room. And yellow is the color of sunshine. For me it's the color of hope!

* * *

Friends, when life gets really difficult, don't jump to the conclusion that God isn't on the job. Instead, be glad that you are in the very thick of what Christ experienced. This is a spiritual refining process, with glory just around the corner.

1 PETER 4:12 – 13 MSG

hospital hair care

Linda Neff

. . . .

Sweet is the voice of a sister in the season of sorrow.

BENJAMIN DISRAELI

ould you like me to wash your hair for you?" I asked my sister.

After a car accident left her confined to bed for three days, Margie looked forward to a chance for some personal grooming. She also marveled that so many people were bringing food to her family and taking care of other details while she was in the hospital. Flowers filled her room. It was not surprising to me at all.

"Relax, Margie. You've been helping friends, relatives, and neighbors for years. Now we're all delighted to have this opportunity to do something for you."

My sister is the kind of sibling and friend that everyone should have. If there is a need, she is there with a cleaning bucket, a paintbrush, and a plate of homemade dinner rolls. A church secretary for many years, Margie kept several ministers organized and free to use their own gifts and talents. Her husband and sons depended on her typing skills to complete most of their university essays. And many good relationships have been started and sustained around her beautifully set table of delicious food.

"I'll be back with the shampoo," I told her as I left to get my travel bag at our mother's house.

Back at the hospital, I carefully wet Margie's hair with warm water as she lay in bed, then I poured shampoo from the plastic bottle. "You have quite a buildup of grease and dirt, so I'm going to wash your hair twice. I didn't get much lather this time." There wasn't much lather the second time either.

"Don't worry about it," Margie said graciously. "It feels so good to have it clean again."

We chatted some more. I glanced over at the side table where I had made a stand-up card. The verse on the card was significant to me: "You gave me skin and flesh and knit together bones and sinews. You . . . were so kind and loving to me, and I was preserved by your care" (Job 10:11–12 LB). We were all grateful to God for keeping Margie alive.

With a promise to visit the next day, I packed my shampoo bottle in a bag. Later, looking through the bag's contents, I discovered what I had used to wash my sister's hair — face cleanser. No wonder there weren't many bubbles!

We both laughed out loud at my mistake. And my sister recovered from her injuries, in spite of my feeble attempt to help her — or perhaps her recovery was partly *because* of my silly mistake. Laughter *is* good medicine! Bonding with someone does not require perfection — just generous doses of being there and doing what we can. And laughing, especially about what doesn't turn out "just right."

· ·

My dear children, let's not just talk about love; let's practice real love. This is the only way we'll know we're living truly, living in God's reality. It's also the way to shut down debilitating self-criticism, even when there is something to it. For God is greater than our worried hearts and knows more about us than we do ourselves.

1 JOHN 3:18–20 MSG

bicycles and butterflies

Bonnie Afman Emmorey

* *

*Prayer is talking with God . . . conversing with him about
all the things that are important in life, both large and small,
and being assured that he is listening.*

C. NEIL STRAIT

Summer in northern Michigan is an awe-inspiring experience. In our town of Gaylord, people say we have nine months of winter and three months of company — and that's not too far from the truth. Our winters last forever, but when summer finally arrives, we forget the weather we endured to get to this grand time of year.

We plan our yearly trip to Mackinac Island to include guests because it's fun to share the experience. The island is historically important, and it's well known for being the setting for the much-loved romantic movie *Somewhere in Time*, starring Christopher Reeve and Jane Seymour, but that's not what draws me back. It's one of the most beautiful islands I have ever seen, complete with exquisite Victorian homes and turn-of-the-century charm. The famed Grand Hotel, sporting, at 660 feet, the world's longest front porch, has rocking chairs overlooking the amazing five-mile-long Mackinac Bridge, which connects the upper and lower peninsulas of Michigan. The island is famous for homemade fudge that melts in your mouth. Trips around the island reveal remarkable rock formations. The ferry ride to the island is always a treat, but the thing I like best is this — no motorized vehicles are allowed on the island. Visitors have to ride a bike or a horse to get anywhere. Since I am a non-athlete, I always rent a tandem bike with my husband. Then I can sit in the back and enjoy the ride.

The year my sister Carol, her husband Gene, and their two granddaughters, Chelsea and Hannah, joined us for our annual trek, my pattern was disrupted. The girls were at that in-between stage, ages six and nine — not quite ready to bike eight miles on their own, but too old for child-size bike seats. The bicycle rental shops offered a creative alternative called tag-a-longs. This invention allows a small bicycle to be attached to a full-size bike and act almost like a tandem. The child on the small bike can help with pedaling or sit back and enjoy the ride. Our husbands attached tag-a-longs to both of their bikes, so that left Carol and me to fend for ourselves. We decided to rent the bicycle-built-for-two. What fun! It would be a sister experience to remember.

Less than ten minutes into our adventure we turned the tandem around and walked back to the bicycle shop. Completely unable to balance the bike, we were a threat to ourselves and to everyone in our path. Carol and I laughed about being such klutzes, but we were unwilling to risk life and limb for the tandem sister ride.

After renting two single-seat bikes, we embarked on the scenic eight-mile trail around the island. It was on this trip that I saw a new side of my sister Carol. Our husbands, with Chelsea and Hannah on the tag-a-longs, were soon far ahead of us. Carol and I leisurely pedaled and talked as we rode. To my amazement, as we biked and chatted, Carol would suddenly start praying out loud, including God in our conversation as if he were riding right along with us. I had never seen or experienced that level of "praying without ceasing" before.

Carol and Gene's son, Jason, was incarcerated and awaiting trial for a serious crime; that situation was heavy on her heart. As we passed couples walking hand in hand along the path, I heard Carol pray, "Lord, in the middle of these devastating circumstances that have caused physical separation in a new marriage, please help Jason and April's marriage to survive, and help them to learn to enjoy communicating with each other in new and creative ways."

As we observed birds in flight, I heard Carol pray, "Father, would you allow my son to one day experience this same freedom?"

When we stopped at the butterfly house and spent an hour sitting and enjoying the remarkable experience of being in a room filled with different types of butterflies, Carol continued to pray for Jason. She conversed with God as easily as she did with me.

As I looked around at the spectacular color and variety of butterflies, I was reminded that they too were in captivity. Their freedom was limited to the walls around them, yet they brought great enjoyment to all who entered. Again I heard Carol's voice in prayer, "Dear God, I ask you to give Jason purposeful living within the confines of the jailhouse walls. Please provide an opportunity for meaningful conversation with a fellow inmate that will enable him to share his faith. Help him to see beauty in the day he is facing."

That trip to Mackinac Island was unlike any I have ever experienced. I came away a different person as I watched my sister share her heart with God. From the freedom of the bicycle ride to the confines of the butterfly house, her spirit communed with God without ceasing, and my understanding of walking and talking with God reached a new level.

My complaints about long winters now seem trite and petty. What a waste of energy! Yes, we are probably facing another long winter, but my heart is filled with memories of bicycles and butterflies, and of a sister who knows the true meaning of walking with God and praying without ceasing.

Be cheerful no matter what; pray all the time; thank God no matter what happens. This is the way God wants you who belong to Christ Jesus to live.

1 Thessalonians 5:16–18 MSG

just patched together

Jeanne Zornes

· ·

Friends are like quilts . . . they are treasures and comforts.

FROM A WALL HANGING

*a*fter forty, its patch, patch, patch," I groaned as Peggy and I cooled down following a heartless aerobics tape. When we both turned forty and noticed the dreaded effects of gravity, we committed to prancing through an exercise tape together at least twice a week.

Peggy is a pastor's wife and mother of three, and finding time in her schedule was like fitting Drusilla's foot into Cinderella's glass slipper. As the mom of two children a bit younger than hers, working a home business, I was just as inflexible. But we fit (pun intended) it in, somehow. From the church gym to her garage (the van parked outside), to the lumpy thin strip I called a "backyard," we jumped off jiggles, lifted leaden legs, and tilted pudgy pelvises. All the while, we complained that the lady on the aerobics tape must have had a caffeine high to push us through agony at warp speed.

Peggy came into my life two years after I'd married and moved to a town where I had to start all over making friends. Peggy was the only girl in a family of boys. I had a sister, but she was nearly six years older, which is just enough gap that when she started dating, I was still playing with dolls. It seemed both Peggy and I craved a close-in-age friend who'd be like a sister. And thus the pieces began to come together.

"Thought maybe you could use these," Peggy said one day as she dropped off a bag of fabric scraps. I sewed most of my kids' clothes and from the scraps made patchwork blankets for my family and for baby gifts. Other times, she came with bags of outgrown clothing for my son and daughter.

Lunches together were nothing fancy. My husband equated split pea soup with green glue. But several times a year, I needed it in my life to survive. Peggy, also a pea soup girl, became my excuse to sneak it into the pantry for quick girl-friend lunches.

When we tired of the aerobics tape, we decided to walk, meeting halfway between our homes and putting another mile on that as we jabbered just as fast as we trotted.

We exchanged babysitting, mending, prayer requests, motherly wisdom, and ignorance. For birthdays, I replaced her frayed kitchen towels, and she gave me a girdle "for those bloated times of the month."

When one Mother's Day she shattered her foot tripping downstairs at church, I took her to the hospital because her husband had to preach. For several months afterwards I went over weekly to clean and do her laundry.

"I'm the only friend who should see your family's underwear," I insisted.

She cared for me when I underwent a breast biopsy. The only problem was the frazzled way she worded her offer: "I'll bring your family some dinner after your *autopsy*." I never let her forget it.

But I felt something die in me the day she made an announcement over lunch at the Chinese deli.

"We'll have to walk a lot farther to exercise together," she said quietly as she poked a fork into egg noodles. "Les accepted a call to a church in Illinois."

I lost my appetite. That was more than two thousand miles away!

What could be my good-bye gift? Not some trinket. I remembered how some of her life's dust-catchers ended up in my yard sales, far away from the original givers. What would be more useful, and more poignant, for her?

Then I remembered. Her old "nap blanket" was a mismatch for the burgundy and green now prominent in her bedroom and living room. I'd sew her a new one, matching fabric on one side to those colors. Patchwork would fill the other side to remind her of her frugal, homespun friend. What better symbol for how two women stitched variegated pieces of their lives into something warm and comforting — a friendship closer than blood.

A decade has passed since Peggy moved away. A few visits and lots of letters, emails, and phone calls have kept the "stitches" of our patchwork from fraying. Her husband is now a denominational leader, and she shares that lonely spotlight. But when we phone or get together, we pick up as ordinary women. "Friends are like quilts," says a wall hanging she gave me and which I placed above my desk. "They are treasures and comforts."

The way we act, you'd think we were sisters. Come to think of it, we are in the same "family" — God's family. For he's the one who pieced our lives together in a tight and fulfilling friendship.

A true friend sticks closer than one's nearest kin.

PROVERBS 18:24 NRSV

sister saves the family farm

Nancy Hanna

Elegant splendor reawakens our spirit's aching need for the infinite, a hunger for more than matter can provide.

THOMAS DUBAY

We call my sister Ginna "the Forrest Gump of the family." Who can forget the image of Tom Hanks playing the role of Forrest, who, through no intentions of his own, became the center of history's most important moments? To Ginna's way of thinking, that's the part she plays in our lives — the central character in the most pivotal moments of our family history. So in hindsight, it was obvious that my sister Ginna would be the one to save the family farm.

Since my earliest memories, my grandparents' farm was the perfect haven for the six of us ruffian siblings during our growing-up years. My brothers baled hay from the meadow, and we sisters learned to cut corn on the cob and snap beans fresh from the garden on Grandma's back porch, in preparation for freezing those vegetables for future family dinners.

Grandma Alliene died very unexpectedly from a brain aneurysm during my sophomore year in college. She was gone from us in a matter of hours. The farm was quieter after that. Once the female nurturer was no longer there as our "emotional interpreter," we got to know Grandpa Edgar better. But years later when Grandpa died, the question arose — what would become of our much-loved farm?

It didn't take long for Ginna and her husband, Chris, to step up to the plate and establish the farm as our summer holiday gathering place for family reunions. And the farm got "yuppied up" too. Sears, Roebuck made way for Smith & Hawken gardening tools and French Quimper dinnerware. My creative sister had the house and outbuildings painted in the country French-inspired colors of butter cream and sea grass green, with a splash of the orange sprinkled in that matched some of the bell-shaped flowers in the nearby field. Ginna frequented farm auctions, and it didn't take long for newly caned chairs to surround Grandma's antique cherry dining room table. The plumbing was still slow and occasionally the well ran dry, but we gladly exchanged these minor inconveniences for the privilege of setting our feet in country grass and for the freedom of running outside in a summer rainstorm in our undies.

Then Ginna masterminded a start-up business on the property. After careful research, she discovered that growing organic lavender was a high cash crop — so she got to work. Or, I should say, our inventive sister put *all* of us to work — watering, cutting, bundling up the stems, and hanging them to dry in the carriage house, buying ribbon, designing products, taking pictures, and designing a website. It took the sweat of faithful husbands, sisters, brothers, a supportive mother, nieces and nephews, along with additional girls and boys from the neighborhood. Sister Ginna dreamed it — and we came.

Yes, Ginna saved the farm. And every Fourth of July you can still find our clan gathering, goofing off, and connecting with each other on the property once owned by our grandparents — sparklers and rockets in hand. We play a mean game of croquet. The sisters can dance up a storm and cook up strawberry preserves at the same time. Ginna is at the helm of our purposeful antics, and we are her worker bees.

At Christmastime I bring magnolia leaves to the Pennsylvania farm from Virginia. Martha hits the Pittsburgh food-strip section for favorite cheeses and gourmet bread. Ginna and Chris order smoked salmon and tins of English biscuits for our festive celebrations. But most important, in these telecommuting, high-tech, media-saturated times, Grandma Alliene and Grandpa Edgar's legacy lives on, and our family gathers to smell the clover, mixed with the scent of Pennsylvania's finest lavender.

When we arrive, Ginna tells us about her latest lavender order on the web: "Some lady from San Francisco ordered eighty lavender-filled pouches for her shoes."

We say, "Who knew?" And then, just as quickly, we chant, "Go, Forrest, go!"

....

Better is a dinner of vegetables where love is than a fatted ox and hatred with it. ... The way of the lazy is overgrown with thorns, but the path of the upright is a level highway.

PROVERBS 15:17, 19 NRSV

going home

Shari Minke

∙∙∙

You keep your past by having sisters. As you get older, they're the only ones who don't get bored if you talk about your memories.

DEBORAH MOGGACH

Our hearts pounded as we walked up the driveway. It had been years since we'd been inside our childhood home. "Hi!" A warm smile greeted us at the back door. "You must be the ladies who called requesting to go through the house. Come on in."

My sister Pat and I didn't get all the way through the doorway before we shouted in unison, "Look! The milk chute!" On more than one occasion, I had squeezed through the narrow passage like a contortionist. I became the family hero when my skinny frame snaked its way into the house, releasing the jammed lock.

As we stepped into the kitchen, memories gushed like rain from a downspout. "Boy, did we wash a lot of dishes here!"

"Ha!" I responded. "Weren't you the one who always had to go to the bathroom when it was your turn to wash dishes?"

"No! *You're* the one who did that!" my sister retorted. Laughter followed.

As we entered the tiny dining room, we paused. This was Pat's favorite room. One afternoon many years earlier, Mom stopped her work in the kitchen to answer Pat's questions about Jesus. Leading Pat to sit by the bay window, Mom asked, "Pat, would you like to ask Jesus into your life?"

"Yes," she quickly responded.

After a simple prayer Mom suggested, "Let's write this date in your Bible. That way if you ever doubt that you belong to Jesus, you can see the date you made this choice written in black and white."

As Pat and I moved into the living room, tears welled up in my eyes. This was *my* special place. On a crisp February morning in 1962, Mom greeted me with, "Shari! Today history is going to be made! A man named John Glenn is going to be the first American astronaut to blast off in a rocket ship and fly all the way around the world. We'll be able to see it on TV in just a few minutes!"

I didn't care about the blastoff. There were questions troubling me. Disregarding my mother's desire to watch the exciting news, I began pelting her with questions:

"Why did I hear you and Dad praying for Uncle Jim so much before he came this weekend?"

Mother quickly responded, "Because we want him to have a personal relationship with Jesus."

"What does that mean?" my five-year-old inquiring mind wanted to know.

Mom turned her back on the television. "Shari, the Bible says that all people have sinned. Sin is when you do something unkind, say something unkind, or even *think* something unkind. Sin separates us from God. God cannot be around sin. God loves us so much that he wants us to live with him forever, but we can only live with God if we ask him to forgive our sins and come to live in our hearts. You know how you get punished when you do something wrong?"

"Yes," I responded.

Mom stayed focused on my face. "The Bible says that God loves us so much that his Son, Jesus, came to earth and died on a cross to take all the punishment we deserve for being unkind. I do a lot of things for you. I cook your food. I wash your clothes. But there is one thing I can never do for you — I can't decide for you if you want Jesus to forgive your sins and be a part of your life."

"I *do* want to do that!" I declared.

Mom and I knelt beside each other. Even though I was very young, I knew that there were times I was unkind to my brother and sisters so I prayed, "Jesus, please forgive my sins and come into my heart." Mom prayed after me.

When we stood up, we knew we had missed the rocket's exciting blastoff. Without any indication of disappointment,

Mom hugged me. "Shari, today you went a whole lot farther than John Glenn did!"

As my sister and I reminisced, the current homeowner listened graciously. With tenderness in her eyes, she said, "I want the two of you to take your time and go through the whole house. Enjoy your memories."

We ascended the stairs to our former bedroom. Suddenly we felt like we were stepping back in time. Our bedroom was *exactly* as it had been twenty-some years earlier! We hugged each other and cried. This was the room where we had shared many secrets, dreams, and prayers.

Holding hands we prayed one last time under the roof of our childhood home. We thanked God for a mom who didn't miss the moments when her daughters were ready to make the most important decision of their lives. Our hearts were joined in gratitude for a mom who stopped her work in the kitchen and stopped watching the television so that two little girls would not just be sisters on earth — but sisters for eternity!

* * *

Daughters, come and listen and let me teach you the importance of trusting and fearing the Lord.

PSALM 34:11 LB

About Carol Kent, General Editor

Carol Kent is a popular international public speaker best known for being dynamic, humorous, encouraging, and biblical. She is a former radio show cohost and has been a guest on numerous television and radio programs. She is the president of Speak Up Speaker Services, a Christian speakers' bureau, and the founder and director of Speak Up With Confidence seminars, a ministry committed to helping Christians develop their communication skills. She has also founded the nonprofit organization Speak Up for Hope, which benefits the families of incarcerated individuals. A member of the National Speakers Association, Carol is often scheduled more than a year in advance for keynote addresses at conferences and retreats throughout the United States and abroad.

She holds a master's degree in communication arts and a bachelor's degree in speech education. Her books include: *When I Lay My Isaac Down, Becoming a Woman of Influence, Mothers Have Angel Wings, Secret Longings of the Heart, Tame Your Fears, Speak Up With Confidence*, and *Detours, Tow Trucks, and Angels in Disguise*. She has also cowritten with Karen Lee-Thorp *My Soul's Journey* and the *Designed for Influence Bible Studies*. Carol has been featured on the cover of *Today's Christian Woman* and her articles have been published in a wide variety of magazines. To schedule Carol to speak for your event, call 888-870-7719 or contact her at *www.SpeakUp SpeakerServices.com* or *www.CarolKent.org*.

Contributors

Charlotte Adelsperger is an author and speaker who has written for numerous publications, including *Focus on the Family, Clubhouse, Woman's World, Stories for the Heart,* and *Chicken Soup for the Soul.* Charlotte gives thanks to God for her twin sister Alberta Heil. Charlotte is a popular speaker at women's events and writers' conferences. Contact her at 913-345-1678 or author04@aol.com.

Traci (T.M.) Ausborn has authored several nonfiction articles. A former church business manager and pastoral secretary, she enjoys speaking at conferences and doing training at the corporate level. She is move coordinator for Providence Health System. Traci makes her home in Camas, Washington, with her husband, son, dogs, cats, and a domestic cottontail named Franchesca.

Dawn M. Baker is a social worker and helps women in crisis pregnancies in the field of adoption. She has been in leadership in women's ministry in her local church for fifteen years. Dawn participates in many facets of music ministry, including the worship team, the kids' choir, and piano and vocal education. She makes her home in Canton, Michigan, with her husband and is the mother of four sons.

Lianne M. Belkas lives in the coastal community of Lynn, Massachusetts, with her husband, Dan. She is one of six children and enjoys spending time with their expanding families. Lianne is a secretary and data entry operator. She enjoys going to the movies with her husband, reading, working on the computer, traveling, photography, drawing, and writing.

Barbara Bond-Howard is a recreational therapist and counts among her blessings a loving husband, three adorable kids, two cats who exemplify "cattitude," a pretty garden, an iMac, many wonderful CDs, a framed collage of Ansel Adams prints, a picture taken with Harry Chapin, and some well-worn hiking sandals.

Joy Carlson is a pastor's wife and strives to bring the creative arts into worship. Joy is the mother of seven children, and her experience with both family and ministry has equipped her to encourage women in matters of faith and obedience. To schedule Joy to speak for your event, contact her at 888-870-7719 or joybells@riverview.net.

Pam Cronk taught elementary school for twenty-six years. She enjoys traveling with her husband and spending time with her sisters. Pam has been involved in crafts of all sorts and enjoys working in her flower gardens as well as serving as the organist for her church. She is now employed in a flower shop part-time, which is her "fun job."

Anne Denmark delights in using her spiritual gift of encouragement. Anne has a master's degree in adult education and a bachelor's degree in child development with continuing education in floral design and clowning. She is a staff trainer with Speak Up With Confidence seminars, and her stories appear in *Mothers Have Angel Wings* and *Tame Your Fears*. Together with her husband, Don, she trains leaders of young married couples.

Jennie Afman Dimkoff is the president of Storyline Ministries Inc. and is the author of *Night Whispers: Bedtime Bible Stories for Women* and *More Night Whispers: Bedtime Bible Stories for Women*. Jennie travels nationally as a keynote speaker and storyteller for women's conferences and retreats. She is also a speaker/trainer with Speak Up With Confidence seminars. Visit her website at *www.*

JennieAfmanDimkoff.com. To receive information on scheduling Jennie as a speaker for your next event, call 888-870-7719.

Bonnie Afman Emmorey is a speaker consultant with Speak Up Speaker Services, teaches communications skills at Speak Up With Confidence seminars, and is helping to launch Speak Up with Hope. For additional information, go to *www.SpeakUpSpeakerServices.com* and *www.SpeakUpForHope.com*.

Brenda Fassett sees every day as another chance to tell a story and have one more cup of coffee. Brenda's testimony includes her steady husband, Doug, and three highly animated children. She has been a seminar and retreat speaker for twenty years, bringing inspirational and biblical talks to life. Brenda enjoys volunteering at her church and her children's school.

Jill Lynnele Gregory lives in the metro-Detroit area with her husband and four children. Jill keeps busy with her children, including a special-needs child, and with women's ministries at her church. Contact her at gregoryfam@wideopenwest.com.

Nancy Hanna is the senior producer of the nationally syndicated TV show *Aspiring Women*. Her short plays appear in two anthologies. A finalist for the 2000 Eugene O'Neill National Playwriting Contest, Nancy's plays have been performed in theater workshops in Dallas, Chicago, and California. Her one-act play *Away the Bear* won the 1997 Regent University One-Act Play Contest. Contact Nancy at nanhanna@sbcglobal.net

Jolanta Hoffmann is a music educator and pastor's wife who loves to direct children's choirs, dramas, and musicals. She is also involved in the church's adult music ministry and is a mezzo-soprano soloist. She lives with her husband, three children, and a variety of pets adopted by the children.

Toni Schirico Horras is a social worker and a stay-at-home mom. She and her husband, Roy, an ER physician, have four sons and live in Oak Park, Illinois. She is the founder of SOS, Sisters of Strength, and the MOB, Mothers of Boys. She often meets with friends to offset the high levels of testosterone in her household. Toni is involved in many ministries in her church. Her passion is encouraging Christians to adopt. For information, contact Toni at toni@horras.com.

Page Hughes is the cofounder of Anchor Deep Ministries. She is the author of *Party With a Purpose*. American Mothers Inc. named Page their National Honor Young Mother in 2003. Page's southern charm makes her a favorite speaker for women's events. For information visit her website at *www.anchordeep.com*. To schedule Page as a speaker call 888-870-7719.

Kelly King is the women's ministry coordinator for Council Road Baptist Church in Bethany, Oklahoma. She also speaks at women's events and conferences. With her background in student ministry, Kelly is a workshop leader at the national Virtuous Reality Yada Yada conferences. She also writes student discipleship curriculum for Lifeway Christian Resources. Contact Kelly at king@councilroad.org.

Sonia Kohler is a public speaker, storyteller, and writer. She has worked for a Fortune 500 company as a seminar leader. She shares stories that bring light and hope to life's challenges. Sonia can be reached at 586-677-8185 or at smcgranekohler@yahoo.com.

Shirley Carter Liechty works as an administrative assistant for speaker and author Carol Kent. She serves on the women's ministry team of her church and speaks at women's retreats on spiritual growth, hope after depression, and grandparenting. Her hobbies are gardening, writing, and photographing her grandchildren. Contact Shirley at sliechty@myexcel.com or call 888-870-7719.

Lucinda Secrest McDowell, a graduate of Gordon-Conwell Seminary, is an international conference speaker and author of *What We've Learned So Far, Amazed By Grace, Quilts from Heaven, A Southern-Style Christmas*, and *Women's Spiritual Passages*. She greatly enjoys giving innovative presentations through her ministry, "Encouraging Words That Transform!" Contact her at *www.Encouraging Words.net* or at cindy@encouragingwords.net.

Shari Minke portrays humorous characters, such as "Norma Lee Crotchety," a feisty, eighty-year-old preacher's wife; "Selma Kidds," a pregnant mom expecting her fourteenth child; and "Liza Little," a precocious five-year-old. Her biblical presentations and inspirational speaking will move you as much as her humor will delight you. Contact Shari at 23870 Greening Dr., Novi, MI 48375 or 248-348-5212.

Elizabeth Murphy is a popular conference and retreat speaker. As a pastor's wife and the mother of four young sons, she finds new illustrations daily. She and her husband, Michael, are native southerners now happily settled in Brookfield, Wisconsin. To schedule Elizabeth as a speaker for your next event, call 888-870-7719.

Linda Neff is the author of *Love, Laughter and Tears — Poems for All of Life*. She works as a facilitator for Speak Up With Confidence seminars and teaches high school English in Guelph, Ontario, Canada.

Cynthia Reynolds served as a missionary in Europe with her husband and three children. She edited a newsletter for missionary women and currently writes "Bequest of Wings," a literary review newsletter. She speaks to missionary families and encourages creativity as a form of worship. She enjoys reading, writing, and all things creative. Cynthia lives in Madison, Wisconsin, and can be contacted at cynkreynolds@charter.net.

Allison L. Shaw is a freelance writer and editor from Sacramento, California. She is passionate about children's literature, her career as a librarian, and her husband, Michael. Her published work appears in *The Sacramento Bee*, several anthologies, and pages scattered throughout the World Wide Web. Contact Allison at allie_shaw@ hotmail.com or call 916-366-3021.

Jeanne Zornes is a women's retreat and conference speaker, and a writer of hundreds of articles and seven books, including *When I Prayed for Patience . . . God Let Me Have It!* She lives in Washington State. Contact her at P.O. Box 4362, Wenatchee, WA 98807-4392.

kisses of sunshine

Hardcover
0-310-24766-7

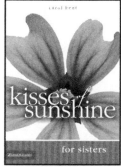

Hardcover
0-310-24846-9

Hardcover
0-310-24765-9

Hardcover
0-310-24767-5

Hardcover
0-310-24768-3

Pick up a copy today at your favorite bookstore!

ZONDERVAN™

GRAND RAPIDS, MICHIGAN 49530 USA

WWW.ZONDERVAN.COM

We want to hear from you. Please send your comments about this book to us in care of zreview@zondervan.com. Thank you.

GRAND RAPIDS, MICHIGAN 49530 USA

WWW.ZONDERVAN.COM